I WAS JUST WANDERING...

I WAS JUST WANDERING...

JEFF LUCAS

CWR

Copyright © Jeff Lucas, 2012
Published by CWR, Waverley Abbey House,
Waverley Lane, Farnham, Surrey GU9 8EP, England.
CWR is a Registered Charity – Number 294387
and a Limited Company registered in England –
Registration Number 1990308.
The right of Jeff Lucas to be identified as the author of this work
has been asserted by him in accordance with the Copyright,
Designs and Patents Act 1988.
See back of book for list of National Distributors.
References marked *The Message*: Scripture taken from
THE MESSAGE. Copyright © 1993, 1994, 1995, 1996, 2000, 2001,
2002. Used by permission of NavPress Publishing Group.
Concept development, editing, design and production by CWR
Printed in Malta by Melita Press
ISBN: 978-1-85345-850-7

Dedication

In loving memory of my dear cousin,
Jeanette Prockter (1933–2012).

Jeanette faced relentless pain with quiet bravery and a warm smile. Always a delight, and greatly missed.

And to Eric, faithful husband and carer, who now lives courageously in the gap. We've been laughing together since I was a boy, Eric, and we've shed a few tears too. Here's to some more happy trails ahead.

With much love.

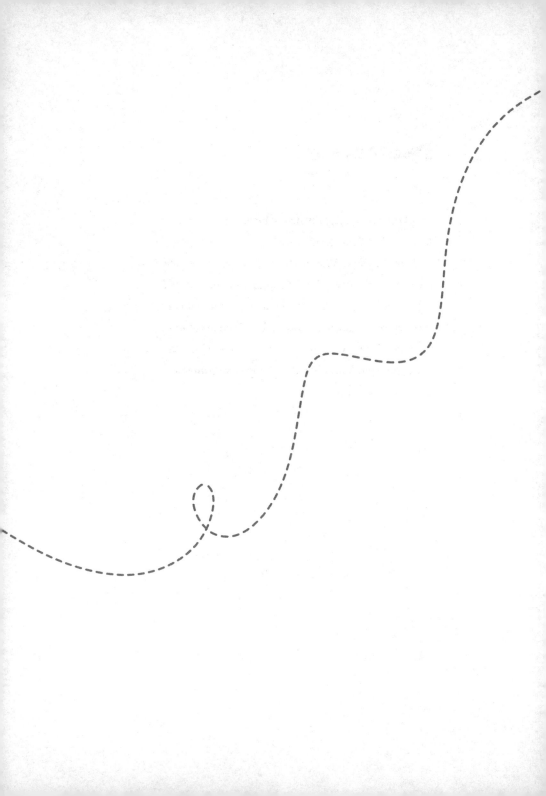

Contents

Preface

It was one of the most memorable sketches that the Monty Python team created. Epically absurd, the sketch focused on the ridiculous notion that government had formed a Ministry of Silly Walks. Gangly city gent John Cleese, bowler-hatted and brolly in hand, strode through the streets of London, limbs akimbo, taking two steps forward and three steps back. Crazy.

Sometimes I feel like my walk with Jesus is just like that. Heeding the call, as millions have, to follow Him, I fantasise about a steady hike onward and upward, a straight-line trek of daily, measurable progress. I dream that there will come a time when I reach the end of a day, and am able to measure my growth in character and kingdom influence. My spiritual development will be precise, able to be plotted on a graph. At best, I will make significant gains; at worst, I might just crawl along faithfully, moving at a tedious snail's pace, but still heading in the right direction nevertheless.

Dream on.

My walk with Jesus is more John Cleese than John the apostle. I envy those speakers and leaders whose lives are a disciplined march; where each of their steps is punctuated by clear directions from heaven, and their days are unremittingly fruitful and exciting. I'm afraid it's not like that for me. My Christian walk is often a Christian stagger. And, sadly, like the children of ancient Israel who, despite the helpful props of a pillar of fire leading them by night and a pillar of cloud by day, I wander. In fact, it's not just that I wander: the old hymn writer was accurate as well as poetic: I am *prone* to wander.

Knowing myself as I do, I understand why God chose *sheep* as a metaphor for the human condition. I wish that God could have described us all as *dolphins* who have swum astray, because dolphins not only smile a lot, but have considerably developed brains, which is why they're good at performing tricks. In short, they can be trained. But sheep aren't so bright. You might go to Sea World, but you're not so likely to go to Sheep World, are you?[1]

And so there are days – and sometimes months – when it feels like I am frantically going nowhere fast. To switch the metaphor from walking to swimming, I'm treading water, learning little, just desperately trying to keep my head above the surface. My primary objective is to avoid drowning. My striding along with Jesus is occasionally punctuated by stop offs at smothering doubt, prayerless speechlessness and furtive little sprints into indiscipline. Sometimes I find myself in the wilderness of despair.

And just when I think that hope is thin, I read the Bible, which is a good idea. There I bump into world changers like Peter, who understood heavenly truths and then came up with hellish suggestions – in the same conversation Jesus congratulated Peter for his depth of understanding, and then rebuked him for being a temporary agent of Satan. In Mark's Gospel particularly, we find a 'warts and all' portrait of headstrong, competitive, deluded, pompous, doubting, irritated and occasionally depressed souls – fellow wanderers, who turned things upside down – or maybe that should be right side up – for God.

And so I hope that you will be encouraged by *I Was Just Wandering*. In the pages that follow, we'll ponder some diverse subjects: low flying golf balls, dementia, the perilous virus of boredom and the dangers of being a highly committed Christian. I'll ask questions about celebrity, believing, and take you to the humid bush of Australia, and the happy town that is Disneyland. Originally appearing in *Christianity* magazine, these pieces have been developed and shaped to produce the book you now hold. I hope you'll buy it.

And if what follows helps you to find hope, and make a little progress in your own life trek, then I shall be encouraged.

Meanwhile, time to move on. Which path now, I wonder?

Or was that wander?

Jeff Lucas

Sussex, 2012

---

1. When I have used this illustration when preaching, some listeners have advised me that there is such a thing as Sheep World, and they're right. However, this doesn't prove that sheep are terribly bright, as instead of walking backwards on the surface of water, leaping through high hoops above the pool and making clicking noises on cue (as dolphins do), the highlight of Sheep World is that the sheep are placed on a track, a dog chases them and one of them passes the winning line first: hardly evidence of brilliance. Sorry, fellow human beings, we're sheep.

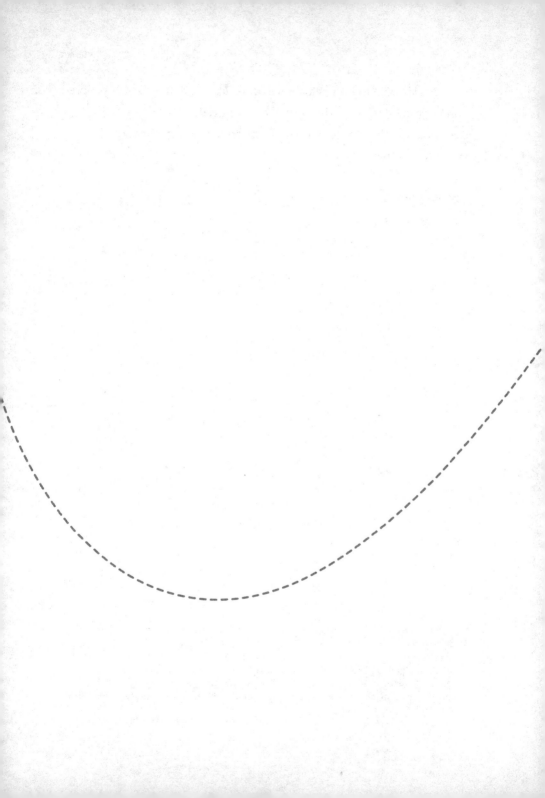

1. I was just wondering

As sins go, it was a minor infraction, if indeed sins are measurable. As far as I know, impersonating a senior citizen is not an offence that calls for a hefty fine or prison time. We were at the cinema taking our grandson to see the latest Christmas flick. He was excited, but the ticket clerk was not only bored, but bad at guessing people's ages. Mine in particular. It often happens. I'm 56, but look older. Kay, my wife, is occasionally mistaken for my daughter, which really cheers me up, especially when she doesn't admit that she's not.

Anyway, back at the cinema, I asked for two tickets for us, and a ticket for 'a little one'. Without looking up, he sniffed a disinterested sniff, and announced, 'Two senior discounts, and a babe in arms.' I stammered that our grandson is nearly three, so is not a baby, but it was too late. 'As far as I'm concerned, he's a babe in arms now, mate. That'll be 18 quid. Here's yer 3D glasses.' The deed was done, the tickets printed. 'Enjoy the film, and thank you for visiting our cinema,' he added in a flat, lifeless monotone that screamed he was just reciting the required script.

And so protesting that neither Kay nor I are seniors was out of the question, M'Lord. The comatose ticket clerk was already so disinterested in life, I feared that even his approaching puberty would be met with a yawn. And so two senior citizen imitators and one baby imitator shuffled into the cinema, plunged our fists into our hot-tub sized popcorn, and perched those ridiculous cardboard glasses on our noses. The lights dimmed, and the movie began. But the clerk's dull indifference draped over me like a wet blanket. And then I noticed Stanley, our grandson.

He was utterly rapt in attention, sitting bolt upright in his seat, eyes big behind those tinted plastic lenses, enthralled. Mesmerised by the cartoon Santa who somehow managed to deliver two billion gifts to children around the world on Christmas Eve, he was transfixed by the unrelenting happiness that oozed from the big screen. He hung onto every word, giggled at the occasionally witty dialogue and stared straight ahead for ninety minutes, his only movement his hand going up and down from popcorn tub to mouth. He was captivated.

Suddenly I felt unaccountably sad. Delighted by my grandson's wide-eyed wonder, I realised that all too soon he would lose it. In a culture where children are forced to sprint towards premature adulthood, his naivety and simplicity will not last long. Innocence will be sent packing by cynicism; reality will thud dully upon him, potentially squashing the fabulous and fantastic for good. Of course, he must know the truth about the world: that children with distended bellies don't get a visit from Santa, or anyone else with food for that matter, and where apocalyptic headlines scream that everything is decaying fast. Reality will triumph, and his capacity for wonder will wither as it does. Eventually, he'll discover the truth about the big chap in red.

Yikes. He might grow up to be alive, but numbingly bored, like the ticket clerk.

But then I remembered that I am a Christian: I often forget. Suddenly I sensed a glimmer of light in my heart, as faint as a distant star in an inky black Bethlehem sky. Wonder is still available, and it's spawned by no fairy tale, digital effect, or Pixar wizardry: it comes from the One whom Isaiah said was called 'Wonderful, Counsellor, Mighty God, the Prince of Peace'.

Wonder came to scruffy shepherds whose only ambition was to see another dawn, and end the cold night chill; they were preoccupied with the numbing business of surviving. Suddenly the darkness fled as the night was lit up in a technicolour, all-singing all-dancing angelic party. Nothing would ever be the same again.

And distant astrologers, their attention grabbed by that same strange star, picked up gifts, trekked some miles and fell to their knees, wonder nudging them to worship.

Wonderful.

And here's the best bit about the story. It's true.

This was no fairytale that offers a temporary warm feeling which fades fast as the lights come up, and we stumble back to a reality that doesn't come with backing music. This is more than the fruit of an imaginative mind, or a skilful screenwriting team, paid big bucks to distract us from the predictability of most of our days.

It's true. We are not alone. Not only is there a heaven as well as an earth, but the two have intersected. Not only have we been visited, but we've been rescued, not by a muscly, swashbuckling warrior, but in the coming of a tiny child.

So let's ask God to renew our wonder, and save us from dulling down the beautiful story. We, the Church, have often taken the magnificent blockbuster and turned it into a tedious third-rate documentary. We forensically dissect our doctrines, and drone our sermons with three points that all, horribly, begin with the same letter. We deliver the message as cold, unappetising slabs of truth. Grace is rendered unamazing, to preachers and listeners alike.

And when the truth about Santa is out, and finally our lovely boy with oversized 3D spectacles realises that no real parent actually called their son Buzz Lightyear, may this truth grip his heart: the kingdom of God has come, and it really is magical, supernatural and revolutionary. Here the good guys get sent packing and the bad guys win because of grace. And the words 'The End' never arrive, because the baby grew up, showed us how to live, and then beat everything, hands down, as He willingly placed His hands on a cross. And the ultimate hairpin turn in the plot was this: written off as dead, He rose again.

Jesus is alive. And wonder lives too.

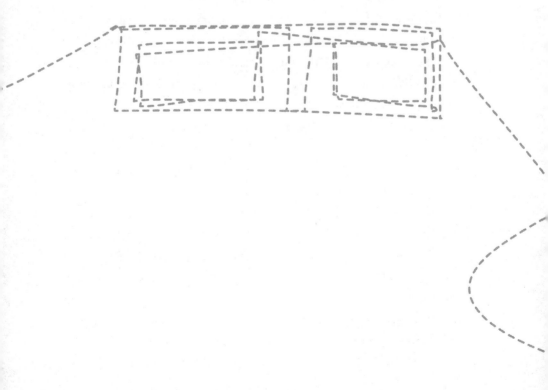

2. Losing my faith

I have decided to abandon my Christian faith.

I'm done with it, for good.

It's over.

The epic decision has been a long time coming, has created a lot of agony and soul-searching, but it is way overdue. I can't keep going anymore. I've talked it over with a lot of friends, most of whom have been understanding and supportive, but I've also kept much of my angst to myself, hoping to delay the inevitable, praying that, like a self-righting canoe, everything would sort itself out. But the boat wasn't flipping, and I was drowning. It's time to abandon ship.

It all came to a head a few months ago. I'm not sure if it was a prayer, or a rant addressed to myself, but the thought went something like this: *I am tired of being a Christian. It's all just too exhausting. I wake up every morning to be immediately greeted by a sense of what I'm not, shaken awake each dawn by the elusive possibility of what I'm supposed to be. I'm overwhelmed by the tyranny of too many 'oughts'. I ought to be a better person, I ought to pray for hours without distraction and read the Bible through four times a year. I ought to solve world hunger, sort global warming and find a way to reach the guy next door, who is lost if I don't reach out to him. I ought to hear God with crystal clarity, be a servant with sacrificial humility, utterly die to self and give till it hurts. And I'm tired. I don't want a purpose driven life. Forget purpose and pack away driven: I just want a life. I don't want to live for a dream, a vision or an agenda. I just want to breathe.*

And so, like a shed skin, my dried up Christianity has been discarded, and I'm hoping not to pick up its scaly shell and try to squeeze back into it again.

Perhaps my announcement of abandonment will create concern, a truckload of tracts and a few impassioned letters from worried believers, urging me to repent, to reconsider, to turn lest I burn. Fear not, and write not.

You see, it's *my* Christianity, *my* mutated form of faith that I'm shaking off and, as I do so, I'm relentlessly pursuing Christ still, asking for faith done *His* way. My problem is not with Jesus: on the contrary. Listen to His words: 'Are you tired? Worn out? Burned out on religion? Come to me. Get away with me and you'll recover your life. I'll show you how to take a real rest' (Matt. 11:28, *The Message*). Jesus is not the reason for my crisis; He's the answer, not the problem. It's my deformed version of faith that I'm divorcing.

Significant junctions in life nudge us to questions.

So I'm asking myself: how on earth did it all come to this? Perhaps, somewhere along the way, I lost sight of this most basic truth: I am a disciple, an apprentice. Apprentices are learners who slowly, painstakingly inch their way to brilliance. They don't initiate, they respond and are teachable. Their role can be summed up in one word: they are *followers*. That was the repeated invitation to headstrong Peter, a man full of words and not so bright ideas, who had to hear himself denying his best friend three times before he could understand what a wonderful, forgiving best friend he had. He had to run out of steam before he could be filled with power from on high.

Followers just do what they're told, no more and no less. Apprentices don't change the world, but cooperate with God as He does. And so, rather than being stalked by what I think I should do, I'm asking to see what He wants me to do. Obvious, perhaps, but a truth so easily missed, at least by me. And here being part of church helps me; I'm part of a Body. It's not me, it's us. Can a finger be an eye? No. I've tried. I'll like to go where He is leading, rather than gallop ahead, hoping He's still around.

And then, in my brand of believing, I had to answer the unfathomable, and figure out the truth of the Trinity, the mysteries of prayer, the reason for evil, the details of heaven, the nature of hell and just exactly why Auschwitz was allowed to happen. In living by the Gospel According to Lucas, I felt the need to defend God when He permitted what I didn't like or understand, like a puny bodyguard for the Holy One, a sentry at Zion's gates. Abandoning my mutant faith calls for more trust, and greater ease in the place of mystery. It doesn't make pain any less painful, but those who suffer won't thank me for trying to explain away their agony with my hollow little slogans.

Perhaps, most important of all, despite preaching grace, somewhere I stopped believing that I am utterly loved and liked by God, just as I am, right now, this very second. That doesn't lead me to surrender to sameness; it's just that I'd like Him to change me by His Spirit, rather than me change me by my sweat. It's not just 'let go and let God'. Cooperation and discipline are still required on my part, but there's a happy surrender to this truth: He's good at making people in His own image, and I am not. A self-made man I will never be.

And so, I bid farewell to *my* Christian faith, and I hope you'll toss your version too. Please God, may it be goodbye, and good riddance.

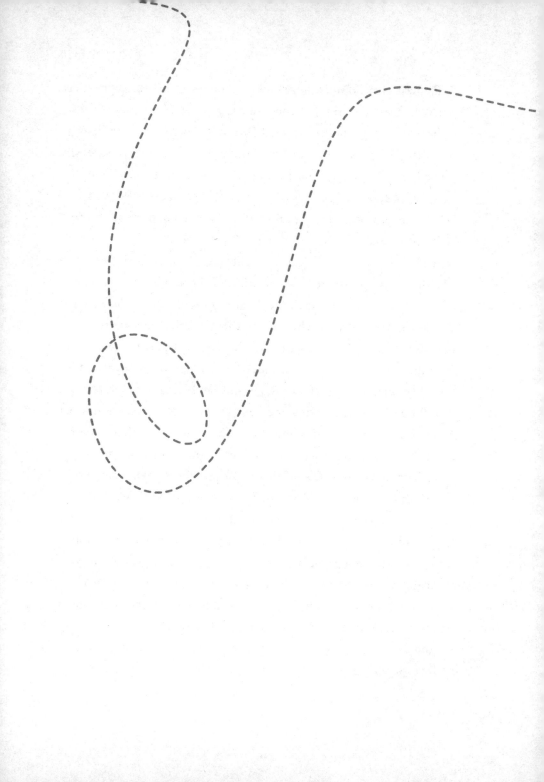

3. Below the belt

I'm not terribly good at hobbies. It's not just that when I relax I feel guilty or because, as a hopeless 'quickaholic', I'm so addicted to rush and activity that I easily settle into play; it's more that my personality demands that I throw myself into any new interest with wild abandon – until I get bored, and then abandon the new pursuit totally.

So it was with scuba diving. I loved the beauty of the crystal clear waters, the fun of avoiding the gaping jaws of Moray eels, the majestic gliding of giant sea turtles. I loved it so much that I considered diving as an occupation, and was thumbing through magazines pondering ads for North Sea Oil Rig divers, while Kay looked on with a wry smile. She knew that my obsession would last just a few days, and then I'd move on.

And I did. But I have never yet moved on to golf. Hoping that I might stay interested for longer than a month, Kay followed up my first visit to a golf course (where I played with a group of Japanese golfers who spoke no English, which was a blessing, seeing as I ruined their game with my ineptitude) with a gift of golf lessons. The certificate still sits in my bedside cabinet, the lessons unclaimed.

It's not just because I'm rubbish at golf; mine is not a swing, more a spasm. And it's not that I think it's ultimately pointless to spend all day trying to use a stick to nudge a ball into a hole, or (even more tiringly) eighteen consecutive holes, while avoiding sandpits. Most sports involve doing useless things expertly and in the shortest time possible, so that's not the reason for my golf loathing. No, the roots of my disdain are to be found in my childhood.

My trauma is superficial. Mummy didn't run off in an electric cart with a chap who was wearing check trousers, their driving off into the sunset limited by the 15mph capacity of the vehicle. Rather, my aversion is due to a rather painful collision between me and a golf ball.

While camping with my family on the side of a course (must get round to asking why we did that), I was walking between the tee and the green when the white cannonball struck. I'm too gentlemanly to specifically describe the area of my body that took the hit, but the arrival of our first child was greeted with great joy and relief. It was a shot below the belt. Literally. Ouch. And so I tend to avoid golf courses.

Sometimes I've been tempted to avoid churches too, because I've taken a few more direct hits since, involved, as I've been, in church leadership. Being passionate people, blessed with opinions, sometimes we Christians disagree, and sometimes we squabble. Disagreement is inevitable, and healthy – it's proof that we're not in a cult, which is good, because I look horrid in orange. But surely we should disagree agreeably, and commit to fight fairly. I've witnessed a few bare-knuckle cage fights, where the saints have gone marching in – with hobnail boots. The apostle Paul had scars that proved his faithful apostleship. I'm short on scars but, like most, have had quite a few bruises.

Christians fight dirty when we make impossible demands that can never be met, as did the lady who insisted that our church wasn't loving enough, a charge that was difficult to evaluate, because there's no measuring instrument available. And even if we did get a bad reading on the non-existent love-ometer, what was I to do about it? I can hardly sprinkle Lucas' 'secret lovey-dovey dust' over the congregation while they're not looking. She seemed blissfully unaware that her own lack of love and grace was not exactly helping us in our 'love score'.

Another kidney punch is the accusation that the teaching isn't deep enough. What exactly is 'deep' preaching? Does 'deep' mean that Tom Wright has been oft-quoted, that a grainy image of an ancient Mesopotamian tablet has been flashed up on PowerPoint, and that the sermon has been sprinkled with a few Greek words, other than *kebab*? Some Christians seem to think that deep teaching happens when they don't understand what the speaker is talking about, as if their confusion is a sign that they are truly connecting with the transcendental. On the other hand, if a complicated idea is presented clearly, they are tempted to believe that the content is lightweight and the speaker is too. Thus, the better the teacher you are, the more likely you are to be accused of not being deep, because you're gifted to make the complex accessible. There's no way to win when that kind of attitude prevails.

Another jab in the solar plexus is the, 'Lots of people agree with me on this' jibe. 'Everyone is leaving the church,' said one permanently offended lady, sniffily. I asked who was evacuating. 'Loads of people,' she said. Who? 'Two or three are going,' she insisted. Their names? '*I am leaving this church*,' she said, as I resisted the temptation to head-butt my tambourine.

But the knockout punch is thrown when we have a fight and we insist that God is the One who agrees with us, He's on our side, in our corner. When we thoughtlessly lob phrases around like 'God has told me', 'God is with me', 'God agrees with me', or (bizarrely) 'God likes the music that I like', we throw firebombs that usually turn a small spat into a world war. Before we were having a rational discussion. But now, in disagreeing with our opinion, others are forced to imply that they don't think we've heard from God, and that we may well be self-deceived. Dissenters become enemies, and calm conversation is rendered impossible. Sadly, too often leaders are the ones who resort to this form of warfare. Feeling insecure, some leaders are too lazy to allow healthy discussion when members of their congregation ask even the most reasonable questions. Suddenly the enquirer is tagged as being difficult, awkward or, worse still, divisive – a threat to the unity of the church. A witch burning is in the offing. This is actually cowardly behaviour, and so unnecessary. It would be easier to treat the question and the questioner with respect, and perhaps even make an attempt at an answer.

So if we have to fight, let's fight nicely.

With that in mind, I'd like to suggest a new practice when the church starts to feel like a driving range. Sometimes we say 'Amen' when we agree, so why not yell 'Fore!' when someone drives an unfair and dangerous verbal shot? That way everyone will know it's time to duck. Or quickly climb into a pair of armour-plated pants.

4. Howdy, stranger

The preacher was working up a real head of steam now, his face flushed beetroot red, his blood pressure soaring. A speck of spittle languished on his chin. 'This is what God calls for, from every one of us!' he thundered, causing me to worry that, at any moment, the throbbing vein in his forehead would burst, which would be awkward, and not a little messy. 'He commands us to be ...' – he paused for dramatic effect, the silence ramping up the tension – '... HOLY!' He paused again, and treated us all to a piercing glare, the sudden contrast between rant and quiet creating an uncomfortable vacuum.

The holy H-bomb shot around the church, ricocheting off hearts and minds, each of us in the pews immediately feeling wrecked and undone. I *really* wanted to be holy. I was *desperate* to be holy, which meant that I would go forward for prayer at the end of every sermon, whatever the subject. My desire for holiness was pathological, neurotic even. There was one problem. I didn't have a clue about what it meant.

So began my lengthy (and perilous) quest for the holy grail of holiness. I became a very confused pilgrim, developing some warped ideas about holiness along the way. I look back on that period of my life with gratitude, thankful that I didn't tumble into a full-on nervous breakdown.

The first casualty on my trek towards holiness was fun, swiftly dispatched on the altar of pious sobriety. Convinced that laughter was frivolous and 'inappropriate', I arranged my face into an expression that implied I was wrestling unsuccessfully with something I'd eaten earlier. My 'frozen chosen' phase didn't last long, but these days I try to laugh a lot, partly because I'm making up for lost time. It's odd that some equate holiness with an inability to smile, or even guffaw on Sunday mornings, but the idea still prevails, surely fuelled by a lingering notion that God is a killjoy, and wants to make us in His miserable image.

Then I discovered – and promptly misunderstood – that verse about 'coming out from the world and being separate'. Not realising that this was about moral and ethical distinctiveness, I dashed into my 'get away from the nasty grimy world and thus become holy' phase, and told my non-Christian friends to get lost, and they promptly obliged. But it didn't take long to realise that Jesus called separatist Pharisees to do acts of repentance, and called grimy sinners to do lunch. I was bewildered, not least because not only was I lonely (my friends having scarpered), but now I felt that I needed to tell the 'lost' about Jesus, and no lost souls were in sight. Now I had to resort to walking up to complete strangers to announce the good news.

Like a 24-hour bug was the brief head cold of legalism I also caught, meaning that I repented of a few things that weren't sin, just to be on the safe side. Legalism is lazy; instead of working out our ethics, we borrow someone else's rules, however mindless they might be. We tell ourselves that we're not lining up with the world's standards, and then absentmindedly get into step with a set of religious notions that are something borrowed and are prone to give us the blues. And legalism deceives; we quietly congratulate ourselves that we are now holy, because we can check boxes on our legalistic list; we don't do this, and we certainly don't do that, so we must be OK, yet we can be totally oblivious to real and huge flaws that are in our character but don't appear on our list. No wonder the apostle Paul told the Galatian circumcisers (a legalistic group, not an ancient football team) to go the whole hog and castrate themselves, which was not a very nice thing to say, but definitely needed to be said.

Then I temporarily bought into that Big Fat Greek heresy, the Platonic notion that the physical is to be avoided in favour of the spiritual. Fasting becomes holy, and feasting suspect. The prayer meeting is to be favoured over the gym. This meant that while on honeymoon, Kay and I dutifully attended lots of church meetings, as if to justify our faltering steps in the land of Eros. Our honeymoon was crammed with lots of lusty hymn singing.

Being holy seemed vital, but elusive. I even got a sense that holiness might be breathtaking rather than musty, and more about life than death, but, like a rainbow, its beauty was distant, fabulous and quite untouchable.

And then it occurred to me that holiness is simply about being different. We're called to be non-conformists, and not in a superficial way. God is different. He's the great Stranger, because He's so unlike anyone or anything. Ancient Israel's neighbours worshipped gods who channelled themselves through warrior males, who sided with the strong, the winners. But Israel's God insisted on standing with the widow, the orphan and the alien. That gaggle of false godettes thrived on power; Israel's God wept and called for justice. The real God cries. Very different.

And so the great Stranger wants His people to be strangers in the world; to live surprising lives that startle. In his first epistle, Peter repeatedly tags the followers of Jesus as 'strangers and aliens'. Being different is tough, because we humans tend to conform; we instinctively run with the herd. But God is looking for an odd crowd, whose ambitions, hopes, dreams, relationships and politics stand out in stark relief, who live the ordinary life in a peculiar way that turns heads, and maybe even hearts. It's a supernaturally natural life, only made possible by walking arm in arm with Him, by faith.

So may God help us all to be holy today. If He doesn't, holiness won't happen. But, helpfully, One of the Three is named in honour of the great cause: the Holy Spirit. Thankfully, He's committed to the journey.

5. You aren't always on my mind

According to God, it's not good for men and women to be alone. Loneliness is torment.

And that means dementia is very bad indeed, because utter aloneness is what it spawns. Dementia is a bullying kidnapper, relentlessly shoving the sufferer into solitary confinement, where the most beloved friends and family gradually morph into strangers. We only know who we are because of who we know. The sight of my child reminds me that I am a father; the voice of a confidante tells me that I am a friend. But when every face is unfamiliar, a blank mask, then I no longer know who I am. This is a bewildering banishment: to be a stranger to oneself.

Dementia is cold and heartless: pitiless, it prises apart bony fingers, refusing to allow its victims to clutch comforting memories of better times from bygone years, or from just five minutes ago.

It dumps those it strikes into a surreal, frightening world, where even the comforting landscape of home turns into an unrecognisable wilderness. This is life in a strange land, an emotional exile, with only thicker fog on the horizon. Fear reigns supreme there. A bump in the small hours or a lingering shadow induces terror because dementia's smart missile is paranoia. Turbo-charging the imagination, it quickens the heart, chilling the blood. It makes the mind its stage, summoning awful, twisted images like a mad Hollywood director; one that makes Tarantino look tame.

Dementia is a monstrous anaconda that silently stalks and then crushes all life in its coils. It stifles, suffocates.

And now someone whom I love dearly is so smitten. Once upon a very long time ago, she gave birth to me, but now she can't always recall my name. She asks the same question, not twice an hour, but sometimes three times a minute. Cruelly, there are times when she realises exactly what is happening to her. The dawn breaks, the fog lifts briefly and her eyes clear. The snake relaxes its stranglehold, just for a while. She apologises tearfully because she knows that her treks to the wilderness are hard on us who watch her insistent trudging. Now she clings onto me for dear life, trembling and bowed before this dementia thug. And she cries and thanks me over and over again for being kind, and tells me how much she loves me, desperate to say it before the mist descends once more on the moors of her mind. Her gratitude brings a strange pain, because I know too well how I've bristled with impatience and tut-tutted over endless repeats. But her words of love fade fast when the snakes squeezes her again, and spiteful words tumble from her tongue.

The serpent flexes its coils, and the sun disappears again for God knows how long. Sometimes it feels like a horrible creature hijacks the dementia victim, disguising itself as them. But there is stealth and cunning too: dementia entwines itself around the worst aspects of the personality. Irritating habits are exaggerated as this vandal disease spoils everything. It sneers at dignity and tramples on it: grey haired, Jesus-loving ladies, once sweet, holy Sunday school teachers, snarl and spew vile expletives.

Dementia. I hate the word. I fear its strike.

So I was shocked to discover that I too am smitten with dementia. Before God's wholeness, I have dementia. Decades ago, Michael Griffiths penned a pithy, prophetic book about the Church, called *Cinderella with Amnesia*. That's what the Church is: a beautiful bride in the making, but one with frequent memory lapses. How often do we ask the same old hackneyed questions, and insist on treading tired, well-worn pathways of sin, always hearing, never learning, seemingly oblivious to the pain we cause God. The incontinence of our sin must surely wrinkle His nostrils, as once again we soil ourselves.

Consider Israel, chosen people smitten with dementia. Over and over again, despite miraculous sea-crossings and manna falling from heaven, hers was the repeated malady described in just two words: 'they forgot'. Stunning moments just slipped their minds. Desperate that they remember, God gave them feasts and festivals, circumcision and ceremonies. Still they forgot.

Nothing's changed. That's why Jesus' parting gift to His friends was a remembrance meal. 'Please, remember Me.'

So today, let's think clearly, learn from our failures and, by grace, live beautifully. Let's allow the memories of sacred moments to shape the decisions that we make. Let's come to Scripture, not just to expand the balance of our information bank, but to allow its truth to shape our lives, our thinking, our reactions. Surely we only truly remember as we apply what we know: only then is knowledge truly learned.

And let's spare a thought and a prayer for the humans who are carers, those who, unlike the Lord of amnesiac Israel, are not God or gods. Do not think that they are strong just because they act as if they are. Let's tread gently around our elders, and never write them off, but treat them with love and respect. They have fought in world wars, but never anticipated that they would fight again for their lives in their fragile years. They had peace in their time, but now their peace is threatened by an unexpected marauder, a new, surprising oppressor.

Let's pray and bless those who are smitten with this cursed dementia, and let them know, with a touch, a smile, a word softly spoken and oft repeated, because so quickly it slips their mind, that they are loved, cared for and that whatever the lying disease might shout, we whisper that they are not alone. Let's pray that the Spirit of God, the One called Comforter, will caress them with kindness: the Spirit needs no words, and can speak life where there is chaos and confusion, just as it was in the beginning, when all was without form and void.

And next time we eat bread and sip wine, and, for a while, remember clearly, let's be grateful for the Great Carer of us all. We cast our cares on Him, because He cares for us. Thank God, He remembers our sins no more, but never forgets us sinners.

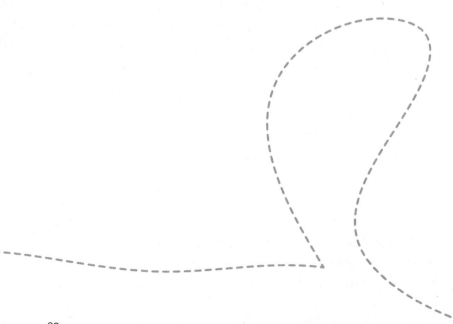

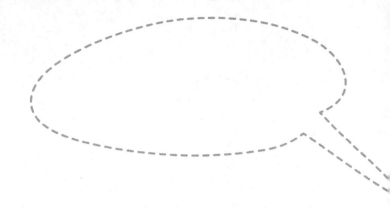

6. All talk?

Evangelism. It's a stun grenade of a word, guaranteed to make Christians feel guilty whenever it's mentioned.

As a shame-inducer, it's like that other word that usually makes us duck: *prayer*. As a preacher, I'm occasionally tempted to imply that I pray more than I do. 'I was in prayer earlier this morning, friends,' I gently murmur, my face a saintly mask, and with one sentence I imply that I awakened the dawn – and the cat – with hours of fervent intercession. Actually, I only muttered two sentences to God while searching for the teabags (one of which was, 'Lord, where are the teabags?'). Crimson-faced Christians cringe, feeling quite undone in the presence of a mighty prayer warrior such as I.

Evangelism creates a similar crisis. We know we've got epic news to share, and so can live in unending neurosis that we're not doing enough to get the word out. My early years as a Christian were spent on the edge of agitation; surely I had to talk about Jesus *right now* with the milkman, the bloke who sat next to me on the bus or plane, all my friends, my family and the lady behind the fish counter in Sainsbury's.

I'd clumsily try to switch every conversation around to eternal matters, which can be excruciating, especially for the hapless pagan. Asked if I'd like a cheese sandwich, I'd affirm that I had the bread of life – did they? Back at the fish counter, perhaps I could ask the lady in the white coat if she had cod, and then ask if she had God, whereupon she'd probably call for some other men in white coats – to take me away.

I went on the offensive, quite literally, lambasting my parents about their dire need for rescue from Armageddon, but never living out the message by tidying my bedroom, which looked like Armageddon. Every conversation became a desperate monologue, as I frantically searched to get to the part about opening the door to Jesus, which must have been quite unnerving for my victims, who were probably searching desperately, not for the door to new life, but for the nearest exit. Have you ever been in the presence of a wide-eyed washing machine salesman who implies that, unless you decide to purchase the Sudsmaster 3Gi turbo with microwave assisted drier *right now*, his wife and children will starve to death? I have. I didn't buy it. And neither did my pressurised friends, for the most part. I blush at the memory.

I even resorted to vaguely fraudulent strategies. Kay and I would knock on people's doors with a couple of clipboards in hand, insisting that we were conducting a survey about religious beliefs, which we weren't. We did write their responses down on a piece of paper, but it was quickly discarded later. We told ourselves that our survey was a means to an end, a way to begin a chat.

But then I did a pendulum swing away from ever talking about God, insisting that I just needed to 'live the life'. Unhelpfully, an instruction attributed to St Francis of Assisi is often quoted in this regard: 'Preach the gospel, and use words if necessary.' This is excellent advice if, like Francis, you give everything you have to the poor, and enjoy happy chats with a variety of animals, thus making your life quite a conversation starter. Lesser mortals like me need to resort to words too.

These days, when it comes to evangelism, I want to be totally available, to listen, to talk, to care. We're not, like the Blues Brothers, on a mission *from* God – we're with Him, on *His* mission. Boldness will still be required, but I want to get caught up in what He's doing, rather than desperately trying to make something happen. Jesus didn't make waves, He surfed the waves that the Father made.

One thing's certain: I'm never going back to thoughtless monologues, where you memorise a script in order to get the message across. Mindless parroting is never good, as I learned when I phoned a customer service number today.

The company that provides my landline (and has been promising me a new internet router for six months) shall be nameless, but I've spent a lot of time talk-talking to them recently. The lovely lady in customer care started into her script. She asked me my mother's maiden name, and my pet's favourite hobby. And then, a question that could win an award for banality:

'Your wife, a Mrs Lucas, is the primary account holder. Is she there with you?'

'Yes, she is,' I affirmed, wanting to say that my wife has been with me for over three decades now, and we're very happy, thanks so much for asking.

'And, Mr Lucas, are you your wife's husband?'

Staggered, I responded. 'Er, yes. That's why she's called my wife.' The script had become patently ridiculous. No one wants to be on the receiving end of prepared statements, or parroted answers. They don't want to become our evangelistic projects, fed into the hoppers of our missional activities. They are not souls to be won, but people to be noticed, heard and loved.

So let's live lives that provoke questions. Let's speak about Christ with kindness and clarity. Let's listen, not just so we can catch our breath before launching into another lengthy monologue, but because we really are interested; we genuinely want to know. To do anything less means we have begun to deal with someone as a project, a prospect, rather than a person.

And when it comes to evangelism, for heaven's sake – let's be more than just talk talk.

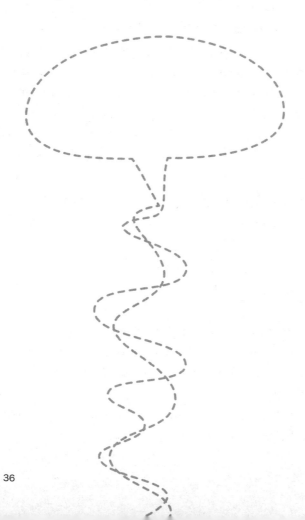

7. Church bouncer

It was a sweltering day in Malta.

Our taxi driver dropped us off in the cobbled town square, surprising us with the delightful news that we could pay him at the end of the day, when he collected us for our return journey: rare trust indeed, and such a contrast to what was to follow. We headed for a local attraction, paid our entrance fees, and joined a small gaggle of people who were waiting for the show to start, only to find that one of our group had mislaid her ticket. She approached the cashier who'd taken her money only moments earlier. Surely there'd be no problem. We'd only just parted with cash.

'If you can't find the ticket, you can't go in. You'll just have to pay again,' said the unsmiling gatekeeper, arms folded intransigently across a formidable bosom, eyes narrowed in suspicion as if we were wannabe ticket touts.

'But we only paid you just a minute ago. You know we did. It's just a mislaid ticket ...'

That lady was not for turning, or opening the turnstile. In her mind, the rules were inflexible: only ticket holders were to be admitted. Even though our friend had just purchased one, she was not currently holding a ticket, and that was enough to exclude her. We fled.

A little later we found ourselves staring up at the stunning edifice of a cathedral, its towering walls and flying buttresses a stunning tribute to medieval ingenuity. Glaring gargoyles stared down at us, grotesque, wide-eyed deterrents of demons. A bell chimed in the tower, signalling that a service was about to start, so we decided to join the gathering worshippers. My Maltese is limited (I can say, 'Pass the Maltesers'), but we didn't want to miss the opportunity to reflect and pray for a while, and to experience worship in this unfamiliar setting. We approached the huge oak doorway, and there met a human, glaring gargoyle.

A stern looking man stood at the door, his arms folded too, just like the unrelenting cashier, his feet firmly planted, his face grim. 'No entry for tourists, it's a service,' he snapped. We smiled that smile which Christians flash when they meet other Christians, and quickly explained that we weren't interested in touring the building, that we were fellow believers, keen to participate in worship. We thought his expression would change, and that we'd be welcomed into the family gathering with a wide smile. We were quite wrong. He made no attempt to disguise his sneer of disdain: 'You don't want the service, you're just tourists,' he scoffed. It took a while, but at last we persuaded him, another reluctant gatekeeper. He reluctantly allowed us to pass with a suspicious sniff. I avoided looking at the beautiful sculpture in the entry way, lest I confirmed his suspicions and found myself ejected, guilty as charged as a tourist.

Red-faced, we quietly took our seats, attracting a few glares from the locals. Song books were distributed, but, incredibly, we were ignored. The service began, a priest's voice a drone, the whole event profoundly lacking any warmth or humanity. And as I sat there, mildly depressed at meeting two glowering gatekeepers in the space of an hour, I realised the source of my sadness. It was not the feeling of exclusion that bothered me so, but rather that we had found ourselves under such suspicion by our two inquisitors. Suspicion had turned them into sentries.

Suspicion is a destroyer of churches, friendships and marriages. It makes enemies for no reason, and turns us into shadow-boxers, fighting imaginary foes. Some people seem to go through life generally convinced that *everyone* around them is suspect until proved otherwise. Suspicion turns us into dark speculators, as we play guessing games about other people's motives. Leaders become nervous and defensive, fearing that a simple question is a vote of no confidence, a potential uprising. And followers can be maimed by suspicion too; tarring leaders with an undeserved brush, they suspect their every move, placing every decision under a microscope, quick on the draw with an allegation, eager to swallow the flimsiest conspiracy theory. Suspicion breeds other relational diseases, like cynicism. The Pharisees, those New Testament religious gatekeepers, were blinded by the two evil twins that are suspicion and cynicism. Corpses came to life, sicknesses were banished and dark forces sent packing, yet these myopic barons did not see.

I've met Christians who are consistently theologically suspicious. Seeing themselves and their version of the faith as the ultimate orthodoxy, they have decided that everyone else is probably unsound, guilty of mild heresy until they prove differently. Disagree with them in the tiniest doctrinal detail, and they'll write you off as a heretic. Given a chance, some of them would apparently be happy to organise a burning.

Dejected, and enduring forty minutes in an unyielding pew that felt like a courtroom dock, we decided to leave the cathedral quietly. And then I took a last look back towards the altar, and it was then that I saw the young man. A lithe thirty-something, with long flowing hair, He was covered in blood. His hands were pinioned by nails, but He was held on to a cross by love. And I remembered that, because of what

He did, the thick veil of 'no entry' was ripped from top to bottom, vandalised forever by grace. A lack of suspicion seems to have scented His life; a woman washes His feet with tears, and dries them with her hair; He trusts her, believing the best. He surrounds Himself with the strange and the sinful, and at last, He entrusts the greatest task in history to a group of feuding, slow-to-get-it disciples. He calls them to believe in Him, but perhaps the greater miracle is this: He believes in them – and us. He was and is the ultimate Gatekeeper, the Way, the Truth, the Life, the Door. And His arms are open still.

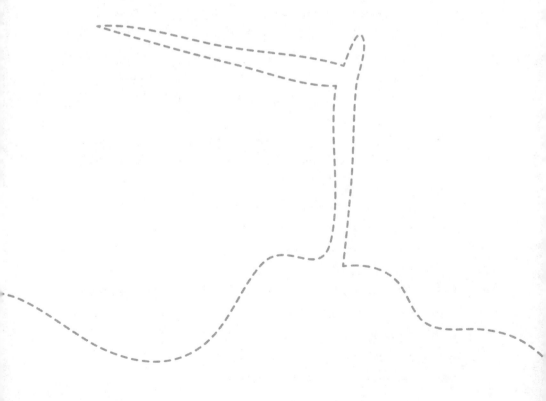

8. Magic kingdom

Having a conversation with a huge, topless tattooed man is quite a challenge. Jim is built like a planet, his gigantic girth covered with manic scribbling, perhaps the work of a tattoo artist on crack cocaine. I tried to focus as we chatted. It's hard to have a conversation with a chap while tilting your head slightly sideways to try to read what's on his left breast.

I had been speaking at a Christian open-air event in a park; Jim had parked himself on the grass and was responding to the blistering sunshine in the usual British way: you remove clothing, mock the idea of sunscreen, pop open a can or three of lager and end the day looking like a poached salmon. He waved me over, warmly thanked me for my talk and then promptly poured out his heart.

I thought that Jim had never darkened the doors of a church, and I was wrong. Many years before, at the tender age of seventeen, he had 'given his heart to Jesus'. A breathlessly excited convert at a church youth camp, he went forward to respond after a white-hot sermon. At first, all went well. Back then, life was simpler for Jim. He had few worries, big dreams and no message to his mum scrawled across his abdomen. But, as he put it, taking another slurp of Heineken, his conversion hadn't 'worked'. He shook his head sadly, wiped his mouth and then, I think, wiped away a stray tear. 'I was expecting fireworks to explode, but nothing happened. I wanted to really feel something, to hear a voice, to bump into an angel. But there was nothing ... so I packed it all in and walked away'.

Now, three marriages and three divorces later, and a string of adulterous dalliances besides, there were plenty of regrets. He'd spent more than a few weekends languishing in prison cells, the only way to restrain his booze-fuelled rage. He shook his head sadly as he surveyed in seconds a lifetime of bruises and bruising.

He sighed wistfully. 'Sometimes I've wondered if my life would have turned out better if I hadn't walked away. Do you think it's too late for me, Jeff?'

And that made me wonder. Perhaps Jim was simply the victim of his own expectations; he just assumed that, if he was a Christian, the pathway would light up before him, daily. But then I wondered if we can be guilty of using vocabulary that makes the Christian life sound more exciting and filled with dramatic experiences than it usually is. There can be times when we sense God walking closely with us, when we see clearly the transformation His Spirit brings. There's no conspiracy here, no intention to mislead – but as we use shorthand and metaphor to try to communicate our faith journeys, we can unwittingly paint faith in sensational colours.

I used to describe prayer as a conversation, until, decades on, I've come to realise that this could give the wrong impression as, most of the time, prayer for me is certainly *not* a conversation.

'God spoke to me this morning,' I announce breathlessly, perhaps suggesting that (a) I awoke to the sound of a booming voice that rattled the alarm clock and (b) I have an ongoing hotline to God and am enjoying happy little chats with Him through each and every day. In truth, 99% of my praying is me doing the talking. Sometimes I get a sense of a whisper, a nudge (and maybe once in a decade or two, something more), but most of the time it's *not* a conversation. In saying this, I run the risk of being tarred as a carnal infidel by some, who'd like me either to focus and listen more, or perhaps retire to the Sahara togged up in a horsehair shirt. But I have to tell the truth about the way that prayer *is*, rather than what I'd *like it* to be.

Something similar can happen when it comes to sung worship. I warble to God that I could sing of His love forever, when in reality I get restless after about 35 minutes, especially if I feel I've been singing the same song forever ...

We can paint a verbal portrait of faith as being like one long exhilarating afternoon in a theme park – all thrills and spills and experiences. And, after a while, we start to believe in the magic kingdom ourselves, as I found out when I went to Disneyland, and actually approached Mickey Mouse and asked for an autograph. Only as I walked away did I realise that I'd just asked a sweating college student togged in furry fancy dress to honour me with a signature. Unwittingly, I'd bought into the myth myself.

Meeting Jim has made me more determined than ever to refuse to airbrush or tart up the Christian walk, but rather to tell the truth about faith, as Scripture tells it. The Bible clearly acknowledges that we don't have a 20/20 vision of God now. One day we'll see Jesus face to face but, in the meantime, it's like peering through fogged-up double glazing.

That's why it takes faith to do faith.

9. MacSmug

I have a confession to make, and it involves sin. Don't get too excited, because there are no juicy, lurid details to follow. The words *romp* and *scandal* won't be used. But I have been guilty, so I'll tell all. I have succumbed to repeated bouts of pride.

It all began when I bought an Apple computer. How quickly this prompted my downfall.

Since then, I have become MacSmug.

I previously owned a PC that was surely possessed by a whole flock of demons (if the collective noun for demons is flock). At times I speculated that my motherboard had been offered to Satan on an altar where young virgins were slain. My PC from Hades stuttered, froze, coughed and, on one occasion, actually screamed: perhaps I inadvertently spilled some holy water into it. That 666 megahertz devil actually allowed me to format its hard drive, and barely warned me of the perils that would result. It was so casual, so unperturbed. 'Are you sure?' it asked me when I told it to delete its own memory, so nonchalant in the face of an irreversible lobotomy. I pressed 'Y', and wiped out my life. The computer ominously silent (it being empty), I decided to provide a soundtrack of high pitched screaming myself. My falsetto anguish was probably overheard in Moscow.

And so, O happy day, I walked into a store resplendent with the blessed logo of the big bitten Apple, chatted with a nine-year-old expert whose badge bashfully announced that he was a genius, and entered the glorious world of Mac. Intimidated by my shiny silver purchase, I left it unopened in its box for a whole year, wishing that there was an Alpha course for those uninitiated in the mysteries of Mac. But then I discovered that there was. Macipleship is offered in the form of a 'One to One' at the temple of delights, the Mac Store. There was personal instruction, with no questions considered off limits, and no quiche eating required. Joy of joys.

But then, alas, smugness crept stealthily into my soul. I began to be sniffy around those who still used PCs, curling my lip with disdain, as if I was riding a Harley in the presence of a Penny Farthing or, worse still, a moped. Soon I joined the ranks of those chortling superior types who roll their eyes when they spot anything made by Bill Gates; my un-PC behaviour meant that I condescendingly offered instant sympathy to anyone with a PC. In short, I became a conceited Macbore. Ironically, what led me to smug superiority was the fact that the Mac is very, very good indeed. (Ooops. There I go again.) I was apparently a better, brighter person just because I owned one.

It can be difficult for us as followers of the One who calls Himself the Truth. Of course, Jesus has the right to so declare Himself, and in a world where relativism reigns (and absolute statements are frowned upon, so right now you might not be reading a book, but are possibly pondering a tomato) the rock solid signpost that is the gospel is a relief in a culture where the road to nowhere is often labelled as the road to somewhere. But revelation can be the pathway, not only to understanding, but also to arrogance. The haughty look becomes a disdainful sneer. The cherished convictions of others become fuel for our mocking.

And sometimes we Christians even get a bit pompous around each other. I've met too many super-disciples who consider themselves to be so spiritually advanced, that church is now way beneath them. Gathering in community with all its joys, pains, frustrations and warm moments is too superficial, too pedestrian for their so cavernously deep souls. Theirs is a potential Gnosticism with a look that says, 'oh dear, if you only knew the heavy stuff we know, your life would be so much better, saddo.'

Whenever we discover something new, or have a junction moment experience with God, we're only five steps away from conceited deception. Our discovery or encounter excites us. It has changed our life, revolutionised our thinking; it is undeniably marvellous.

And so, fuelled with high-octane exhilaration, we begin to share what we've found with others. They need to read that book, we insist. If they'd just attend *that* conference or taste what we've experienced as so utterly life-changing, they'd surely be the better for it.

Suddenly, we meet resistance. Our breathless sharing is welcomed by some, and appraised and even rejected by others. We're disappointed now, even a little hurt. Maybe we're hurt quite a lot. We smart at the realisation that all are not buying into what we so quickly bought.

So now we begin to try to consolidate our position. We only attend the conferences where speakers who are from our crowd speak. We only read books that are published by our theological or experiential clan.

And then, when we gather together for warmth with those enlightened souls who agree with us, we begin to think of ourselves as those in the know. We look down with sad pity at those who have not seen what we have seen, who don't know that we're in the know, who are not as blessed as us, anointed as us, deep as us, radical as us. We dismiss those who try to dialogue with us as sad, irrelevant types. We will not be deterred, we insist.

Hey presto. We've gone from revelation and encounter to smug deception in five easy steps.

So when we're around people of other faiths, or no faith at all, let's be sure to offer a listening ear rather than a masterly monologue. Let's treat their stories with the respect that we hope they'll give ours. When we're tempted to believe that we're first-class believers while other Christians are just stranded back in their minuscule economy-class seats, let's remember that the same grace has rescued us all; whatever we have, we've been given; whatever we know, we've been shown. The disciples who tear up their 'L' plates may have graduated in their own eyes but, in truth, have simply abandoned their apprenticeship.

And if humility is hard, then just remember this: each of us has been tainted by the taste of another bitten apple, nestling in the branches of a tree in Eden's garden.

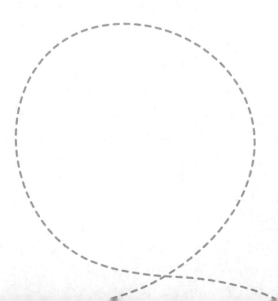

10. Creating a culture

It was a day of stark contrasts, in which I witnessed crassness and grace, and all in the same hour.

Travelling by train to Nottingham, I had found myself shunted into an emotional siding of despair. Disgust isn't a word I often employ; it sounds too shrill. But disgusted I was as I endured the conversation of five chaps who sat across from me on the juddering train. Adolescents disguised as middle-aged men, these forty-somethings on an outing, each one of them clutching a can of beer in hand, loudly filled the carriage with putrid chatter. And it wasn't just the endless bad language that jarred. They leeringly boasted of their (probably imaginary) exploits with women, whom they obviously viewed as objects to be used rather than people to be cherished. Like a bunch of college kids out on the razzle, they described in dank detail their boozy nights and vomit-soaked awakenings. I've said enough about their conversation; to report any more would stain your mind and likely turn your stomach, as it did mine. I kept glancing over at them, offering a quizzical look that might perhaps nudge them into embarrassed silence, but it was in vain. I nervously decided to stop my glaring; the more they drank, the louder they became, and I wondered if they might add violence to their collection of dubious accomplishments; violence towards me in particular, if they decided to wipe the shock glare from my face. Other passengers wrinkled their nose in disdain, and hunched lower behind newspapers in an attempt to shield themselves from such ugly talk. I seethed.

It's been said that we're living in a culture where children are being forced to grow up faster and where people are maturing more slowly. Certainly these beer-belly-sporting overgrown teenagers were testimony that this is true. All seemed gloomy as they sought to shock each other with their woeful tales.

Arriving at Nottingham at last, I lugged a heavy case and a heavier heart out of the train, overwhelmed by the fear that Britain is becoming a crass, fetid culture. Coarseness is too commonplace; men and women behaving badly comes as no surprise. It's the way things are. We lament the condition of our culture, but feel powerless to do anything to help repair it. However, we're quite wrong to wring our hands in despair, and feel we can't change anything. A few minutes later, unexpectedly, the sun came out.

With fourteen miles to go to get to my hotel, I decided to take the bus. And it was then that hope dawned once more.

The bus was a few minutes ahead of schedule, so I was able to ask a few questions of the driver about the route as he waited for his departure time. He smilingly told me everything I needed to know. And then a young man, standing in the queue, chimed in helpfully. Here I blush: the lad was so friendly, I thought at first that he had some special needs. Some of the most kind, loving and expressive people I meet are also those who struggle with learning difficulties; they are free of the social hesitation that paralyses so many of us who tag ourselves as 'normal'. How tragic that I would think that someone as kind as that young man might have to face unusual challenges in order to be so lovely.

And then the bus journey began, and I watched a startling, warm drama unfold. At every bus stop (and, during the hour journey, there were many) the driver turned to smile at and thank each departing passenger. They, in turn, nodded and verbalised their thanks. One or two more ominous looking types, who were snuggled menacingly in hoodies, shattered my prejudice as they spoke out their thanks to him, loud and clear. In a cold, anonymous world, this man was creating a culture of beauty on his slow moving bus, as he took the time to notice and acknowledge each passenger as his guest.

And the lad who had been so kind in the queue? He went up and down the bus, picking up litter and ensuring that vehicle stayed pristine. Without being asked, he hastily vacated his seat for a lady who boarded, offering it with a smile. And then, discovering that I was a newcomer to the area, he gave me a little guided tour as the bus meandered around the town. To be honest, he pointed out sights that were not really epic, but I was grateful for his thoughtfulness:

'That's Lloyds Bank ... and the Fire Station ... and the Chinese takeway ... and the Post Office ...'

When we finally reached the stop nearest my hotel, our kindly tour guide helped me from the bus with my gigantic case. Living as I do in America, I reached for some cash to tip him, but it was too late. With a smile and a wave, the bus was gone. And so was the sense of despair that had seeped into my soul back on the train.

Our words, our attitudes and our small acts of grace create a culture around us. When we gossip, we give permission for gossip. A smile might well beget a smile.

Crassness is catching. But, thankfully, grace is catching too.

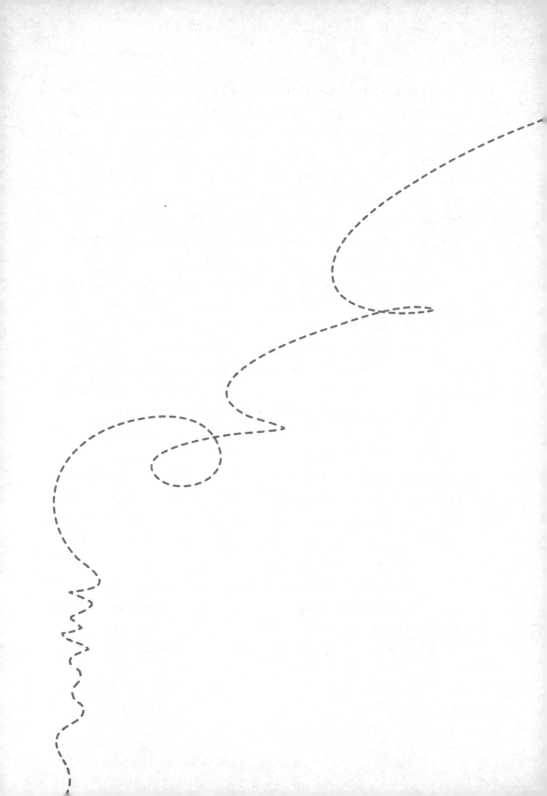

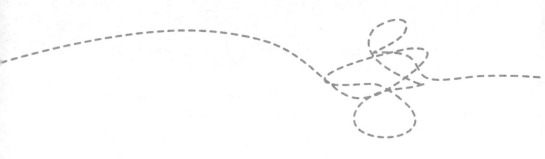

11. Blessed bee

I am blessed to be a bee.

Not literally, of course. Real bees are rotund, wear stripy jumpers and sometimes sting. But my ministry calls for me to cross a lot of denominational lines, and so, like one of those humming types that spends life sipping nectar from a variety of buds, I am a bee. And I've imbibed so much as I've flitted around the tribes.

My Anglican friends have taught me about the solidarity and beauty of liturgy. Sometimes life renders me speechless. To declare faith with well-worn, tried and tested words, uniting my voice with others, whatever the weather, brings an unexpected strength to my charismatically 'spontaneous' soul. Sometimes I use *Common Worship* in my own personal prayers. Because the liturgy is responsive, I have to play both parts: 'The Lord be with you,' I say. 'And also with you,' I tell myself. If this seems strange, fear not. I use different voices. Once I despised tradition, confusing it with traditionalism. Dismiss it as the fruit of ageing if you will, but these days I see how priceless is the practice of holy habits. And I envy my Anglican friends because of their dutiful journeying through the Christian calendar. I don't know my Epiphany from my Michaelmas, but I believe that treating the seasons as reminders of the big story is a magnificent idea, one birthed in the heart of the God who gave Israel their feasts and festivals.

The Baptists have taught me the significance of the baptismal vow, and the Salvation Army has wonderfully unsettled me with their blood-and-fire passion for the poor. My Pentecostal friends have a healthy disdain for religion taken mild, and have a winsome sense of anticipation for what the very much alive God might perhaps do. And I was calmed by a weekend spent with a group of Mennonites, who carried a sense of peace that was tangible. My racing pulse seemed to slow while I was with them. I still shed a tear when I remember their sung farewell to Kay and me: 'God be with you till we meet again.'

But my latest cross-denominational foray led me to a group of happy Methodists in Northern Ireland. The visit included an unusual sighting of sunshine in an Irish August, and involved eating mountains of fine puddings with lashings and lashings of creamy custard. The chairman of the conference blessed everyone with jokes that were so bad that they were good. The nightly announcements were punctuated with puns and chortles.

Yet the Methodists of Castlewellan helped me to do more than gain weight and giggle. They gave me insight into a challenge that I've been pondering for a while. And that's the call to follow Jesus in the *now* of my life.

When I decided to become a Christian, the universe was a different place. Remarkably, a mullet was still loosely regarded as a hairstyle. It being the seventies, a fashion demon roamed the earth, and clothing was garish and horrid. The Bay City Rollers wailed. Something called Crimplene was worn, as was Bri-Nylon. Curtains were made of velvet, as were some men's jackets. Lapels were wide, platform heels were high, and (impossibly) Noddy Holder was young. And so was I.

My name was Jeff, I was seventeen, and I was very different from the person I am now. Scratch different. I was unrecognisable. Back then, I 'gave my life' to Jesus. But the life I gave Him was that of a carefree teenager living with his parents and still in high school; the life that I gave Him was uncluttered by mortgages and bills. It was a life that was naive and simplistic. I played guitar in a rock band, and wanted to be a professional musician, despite only possessing ten or so chords. Make that nine. I was the lead singer, an amazing fact, considering that I now know (having once been a worship leader) that when I sing, people cry out to God. In despair.

I'd been working in a Marxist theatre company in London, and was enamoured by rumours of a revolution to come. Mine was a young life that was idealistic, passionate and trusting. The person I was, swallowed everything that was taught him, often without chewing it first. It was a life high on enthusiasm and light on wisdom.

When I became a Christian, I honestly thought that the way my church, my denomination, did faith, was *the* way. How grateful I am that the man who was my pastor back then quickly began to introduce me to other believers from other tribes. Slowly it dawned on me: I had so much to learn from them. They saw things differently, did things alternatively. *Our* way was not *the* way. I was beginning to become a bee.

And so the life I offered to Christ then is not the life I have now. Now, I am heading at terrifying speed to a birthday with the number 6 at the beginning of it, which is a surprise to me. Like most of us, I still feel like an eighteen-year-old trapped in an ageing body, who wonders what on earth has happened. It is a cliché to say that life is quick, but let me say it. I was unprepared for what took place in just 132 months of my life. One day I was thirty-nine, a relatively young man flourishing in his late thirties. Just eleven years later, I woke up to discover that I was now a man in his early fifties. In a little over 500 weeks everything changed, the rudest of awakenings. I am utterly different.

Therefore reevaluation is needed. I'm not suggesting that I need to become a Christian once again, every decade, but rather consider what it means to follow Jesus as the person I've become. And that's where those happy Methodists helped me.

At the beginning of every New Year, they participate in a covenant service. The liturgy is sobering, as annually they renew their vows:

'I am no longer my own, but Thine. Put me to what Thou wilt, rank me with whom Thou wilt. Put me to doing, put me to suffering. Let me be employed for Thee or laid aside for Thee, exalted for Thee or brought low for Thee ... And now, O glorious and blessed God, Father, Son and Holy Spirit, Thou art mine, and I am Thine ...'[1]

So here is my pledge, made once more. My name is Jeff, I am fifty-six, and I am a follower of Jesus. Now.

And I am a bee, and better for it.

1. From John Wesley's 'Covenant Prayer', British Methodist Church, 1936. Used with permission.

12. Health warning

The service is over, the musicians are packing away their gear. Gaffer tape is ripped from the floor as the PA is dismantled. The man approaches me, nervous. He looks this way and that, like a furtive criminal fearing capture. He has the eyes of a fugitive. He shakes my hand, his grip not too firm, his palms sweaty. 'Could I ask you a question, Jeff?' he hisses, embarrassment flooding his face crimson. I wonder what terrible secret makes him so uncomfortable, as he shifts his weight uncomfortably from one foot to the other.

'Is it OK for me to say that I've got a headache?'

I pause for breath and thought, surprised, but I immediately know the source of his shame. He comes from a church where Christians are simply not allowed to be unwell. For them, sickness is a sign of defeat. All manner of maladies, be they haemorrhoids or halitosis, colic or cancer, are enemies from hell, dark invaders to be routed by the courageous soldiers of faith. He has been told to 'confess' that he is well when he isn't, to take control of his body with positive words. The mad notion is that God spoke the universe into being with powerful words, and so now His followers can create their own reality in general – and health and prosperity in particular – by the power of their words spoken. Like all effective heresies, this one is simply a matter of exaggeration. We *do* speak words that are powerful when we come to the place of prayer and ask for that kingdom of His to come, for His will to be done, but to suggest that we can use words like little 'goddettes' is a gross distortion of that truth. Yet this is what my nervous new friend had been taught. If he kept saying he was well, then well he would be. And so to admit that he has a headache is tantamount to hoisting a white flag of surrender.

I reply. 'Well, without sounding like Julie Andrews, let's start at the very beginning. Do you have a headache?'

He lowers his eyes, ashamed, like a cowardly deserter.

'Yes.' And I sigh because, due to bad teaching, he has a headache and heartache both.

I believe that God still heals. Healing grabbed my attention before I became a Christian, although the condition that I was freed from wasn't exactly epic. After praying, a cluster of verrucas disappeared from my right foot overnight. The blockbuster testimony book *Victorious over Verrucas: How I was blessed with a brand-new sole* won't be appearing at a Christian bookstore near you anytime soon. As signs and wonders go, it was more of a 'wonderette'. But I went to church to try to find out who had sorted out my foot. It was a small miracle that led to the greater miracle of my turning.

I utterly believe in divine healing, and long to see more, because being seriously unwell hurts in more ways than one. Pain has no adequate vocabulary to express its depths. And long-term sickness isolates as well as debilitates; sufferers can feel like outsiders because of their condition. They can feel like cases rather than people.

But we can sprinkle salt into already gaping wounds with some of our 'Christian' responses to sickness. The person in a wheelchair is told that they are permanently seated because of personal sin in their life. This crass generalisation is itself sinful. While there is a root connection in Scripture between fallenness and all sickness, and a couple of instances where sin was the specific reason for a condition, the Bible drives a truck through the notion that this is always so.

And then there's the mad notion of 'seed faith', particularly beloved by television evangelists with large broadcasting bills to pay. The idea is that 'faith' is demonstrated by parting with cash. Not only is this ludicrous ('… and Jesus was unable to do miracles in that place, because nobody had a Visa card available …'), but it is in fact a tarted-up system of indulgences, and one that our ancestors in the dark ages saw through.

But this week I discovered a brand-new piece of quackery. A lady who was battling breast cancer was telephoned by a Christian 'friend' who had recently attended a healing seminar.

On hearing that the problem was with the left breast, the friend told the cancer sufferer that the seminar had revealed that her illness was caused by her 'terrible relationship' with her mother-in-law, whom she should forgive immediately. Incredibly, she went on to say that cancer in the right breast would indicate that she had problems with her mother. 'My mother-in-law is dead now,' the cancer/naff theology victim told me, 'but I adored her. She was one of the most beautiful people I've ever met. We had a great relationship.'

Think about the fruit of that so-called seminar. A wonderful, now deceased woman could have been maligned, the hapless accused in a charismagic courtroom. If the relationship had been difficult, unjust blame could have been levelled. And as the advice implied that forgiveness more than chemotherapy was needed, an unnecessary death might have been the final result.

Let's affirm that God heals today, but admit that it doesn't happen as much as we'd like. Let's know that a theology of healing demands that we wrestle with a theology of suffering. And let's ask tough questions when someone has a 'revelation' about healing.

Because some teaching on healing should definitely carry a health warning. It might be a matter of life and death.

13. From here to eternity

When I was a bright young Christian thing, heaven was a hot topic, as were all things related to the second coming of Jesus. We talked breathlessly about the 'signs of the times', and devoured books that yelled that the end of the world was very nigh, most of them written by Americans who claimed uncanny insight into the future, but seemed oblivious to their own bad hair.

We were hopeful and nervous in turn; keen to meet Jesus, and yet fretful about the possibility that everything on earth might be wrapped up prior to us being married – and having sex. We clutched 'prophetic' charts printed in lurid gothic lettering that (wrongly) turned the book of Revelation into a timeline; we speculated about the identity of an alleged antichrist figure. Lenin, Mussolini, Hitler, Stalin, and Henry Kissinger were considered as possible candidates for beasthood, as we played the popular eschatological game *Name That Antichrist*. Even Bob Dylan was briefly considered for the role until he messed up the theory by announcing himself to be Christian. The second coming was like a real-life unfolding drama with a cast of characters that kept changing. The books on the second coming kept coming back too, reprinted in multiple editions with some cast members' names deleted and with a few new additions to the beastly list.

We wondered what heaven would be like, and struggled with the clutter of unbiblical notions of fluffy pink clouds and androgynous looking angels, harps in hand. I was privately concerned about boredom, because heaven sounded alarmingly like an endless prayer meeting. During one stunningly numbing service, when we sang the same song twenty-seven times, and sensed that watching angels were tearing their flowing blond hair out, the worship leader informed us that heaven was going to be just like this, only longer. Yikes.

Sometimes the neurosis turned into full-blown madness, like when an alleged NASA scientist called Edgar Whisenant published *88 Reasons Why the Rapture Will be in 1988*, calling the world to be expectant, faithful and ready. He sold 4 million copies. When our Lord didn't oblige by returning, the hapless Edgar did a comeback himself with a revised prediction that it would all happen in 1989, perhaps suggesting 89 reasons for his theory, one of which might have been that Jesus didn't show in 1988. Incredibly, some had their pets put down in anticipation, wanting to spare their spaniels and tortoises the rigours of the Tribulation, and many ran up huge credit card bills, believing that they wouldn't be around to the pay them, a highly dubious legacy. Of course, Jesus didn't return in 1989 either – I expect you know that. I don't know what Ed did with the rest of his life. He was last heard of in Hawaii, perhaps being faithfully expectant and ready on a beach.

Our preoccupation with the end times prompted some silliness. But I've wondered if the pendulum that so often swings in the Church has yet swung again, and we have forgotten our future. Is it possible that we know full well that the kingdom is now, but the fact that it is not yet has slipped our minds? Have we lost our grip on eternity?

Today I had to remind myself of the Christian hope, in a moment of crisis that I didn't anticipate. I was watching a film that included a scene where a father and son were enjoying each other's company and, despite my own father having died over thirteen years ago, I was mugged by a crushing grief, and felt the sharp sting of death. I suddenly missed my dad with an unbearable sadness that quite literally took my breath away. For some moments I felt paralysed by a sad claustrophobia; I felt trapped, sealed up in the now, where my dad is not, quite unable to get back to then, where he used to be, alive and well. Without the gospel, he is gone forever, never to be seen or heard of again. Tears running down my face, I told myself that there will be a reunion. I confess that, for some seconds, it felt like pie-in-the-sky wishful thinking, a flimsy notion to cling to for comfort, but I affirmed my hope of heaven and my conviction that one day I will meet Jesus, face to face, when heaven finally comes down to earth, the new Jerusalem. I'm convinced we need to talk far more about the spectacular future that is ahead.

And of this I'm also persuaded: there will be a moment when I bump into a grinning chap with a cockney accent, and the hugs and laughter and back-slapping will begin. There will memories recalled and celebrated, and lessons learned along the way shared in that day of reunion.

Who knows? Perhaps I'll introduce him to you, and we'll have a cup of tea, for surely heaven wouldn't be heaven without tea. Perhaps he'll tell you his story; he always loved to talk, and surely even death hasn't changed that.

I'll look forward to it. You can call him Stan. I'll call him Dad.

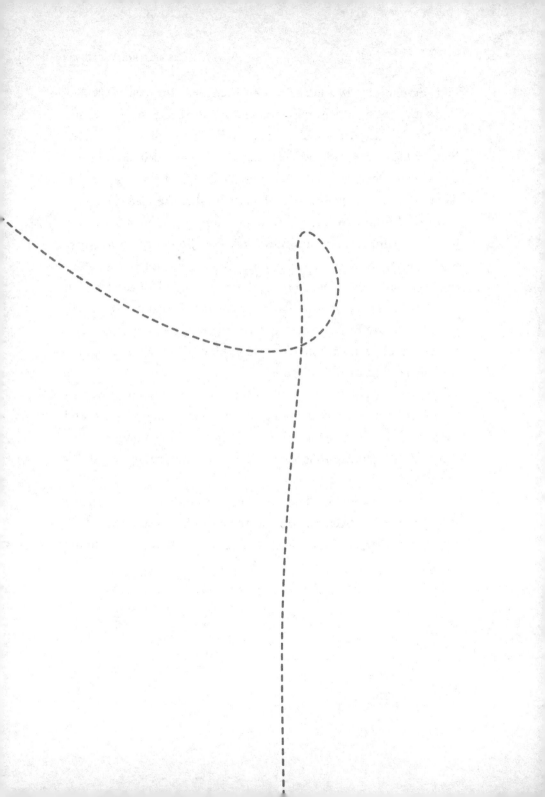

14. No more Mr Nice Guy

Jesus is not nice.

Put that brick down, please. Lest I be forced to appear on the Christian gameshow *Stone That Heretic*, let me clarify. Jesus *is* love, perfectly personified. He is unfailingly kind, staggeringly generous and utterly good. But nice He's not. We shouldn't mistake niceness for Christlikeness.

'Nice' is a word often used of waffling, impeccably pleasant English gentlemen who wear tweeds and sport a monocle. It can conjure an image of a Jesus who sports a sickly smile and, as a fashion choice, wears a stricken sheep as a scarf. The nice version of the Son of God is proper and polite. He knows which cutlery to use at the dinner table, but turning temple tables over would not be for Him. Too much fuss. Quite unseemly.

Nice people don't share rugged conversation, but benign niceties. They're usually found nodding in agreement or being silently non-committal. Nice husbands insist, no darling, your bottom doesn't look big in that, knowing that seams are straining and, alarmingly, may give way at any moment. The nice congregational members compliment the sermon as 'deep', when deep was actually the sleep that it induced; the tuneless solo was beautiful, they say, when everyone knows it was agonising. Angels were sporting earmuffs, and not because of the cold.

Nice people silently watch as their friends meander into mad choices; patting them on the back, the mantra of the nice is 'It'll turn out alright' or 'I'm sure you're right', tiptoeing nicely even as those around them stomp off into obvious disaster. Compulsively nice people sometimes shirk their responsibilities; worried that a contrary opinion might upset the apple cart of a church meeting, they refuse to rock the boat, which ends up sinking, holed by (I can't resist it) a *nice*berg.

The nice can easily be victimised. Frantic to please, they bow in limp compliance without a whimper of protest, and can be vulnerable to herding by an unscrupulous leader, or, even worse, abuse.

And so nice doesn't work to describe the real Jesus. He talked straight – sometimes alarmingly so, tagging religious VIPs as vipers and whitewashed tombs. He did what He needed to do; nice people go with the flow, living constantly in the surging current of other peoples' expectations and preferences. But when His apprentices tried to manage Him, and set to send the mother and babies group away, Jesus blessed the babes and got indignant with His wannabe minders.

Peter even tried to cancel Jesus' terrible appointment with the cross; but far from quiet acquiescence, Jesus rejected Peter's notion by nicknaming him 'Satan', a somewhat blunt strategy, and certainly one that isn't nice.

I'm certainly not suggesting that Jesus was and is a crass, insensitive macho type. Recently I heard a speaker say that Jesus was a 'man's man', which was a relief, he said, because he could never worship a Saviour that he could beat up, which is incredible. This suggests that real men only respect and love those that they can take in a fight, a bizarre portrait of masculinity. Jesus is the Lamb of God who *did* allow Roman thugs to beat Him up, and skewer Him to a cross as well. That said, we must reject an airbrushed glossy pic of Jesus: Dorothy Sayers laments, 'We have very efficiently pared the claws of the Lion of Judah, and certified him "meek and mild", and recommended him as a fitting household pet for pale curates and pious old ladies'.

And I'm certainly not sanctifying rudeness. We've all met Christians who live on a destructive safari, endlessly hunting others down, to 'speak the truth in love' to them. I've met a few of these truth-lovers, and often what comes out of their mouths is neither truthful nor loving. Perhaps, like me, you've bumped into the sterner types who are like stage prompters sitting in the wings, forever correcting our every word. 'God bless you,' I say, meaning it. *'He does!!'* they insist, rendering my comment worthless and unnecessary, thank you very much. More rude Christians are not required; sadly, there isn't a current shortage.

No, let's be gracious, thoughtful and, when we speak our minds, make sure our brains are switched to *on*. May love, not being seen to be right, be our motive. Let's give permission to others around us to tell us what we don't want to hear, even if our bottoms actually look huge in that. If we react with a rant when they tell us the truth, then we'll end up with only the mirror as friend; we're the fairest of them all, and lonely with it.

Kindness, not niceness, is what's called for.

Of course, all of this is easier said than done. Yesterday I asked my wife, Kay, a question: 'Am I becoming neurotic?' She laughed out loud, and I waited for the welcome reassurance, which didn't arrive.

'What do you mean, *becoming*?'

Not nice, even if true.

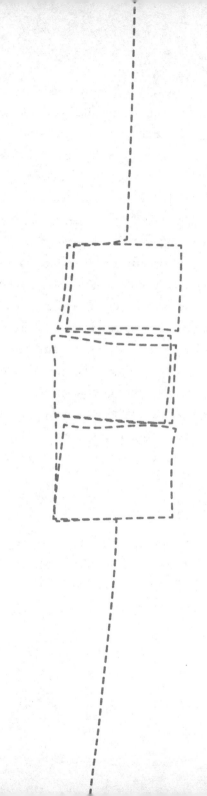

15. Straight talk

OK, so my passport photograph isn't the best. Actually, it's really quite scary. I'm not sure what I was thinking when I popped behind the green curtains at the booth in the now defunct Woolworth's, fed my pound coins in and then glared like a trainee serial killer into the glass square that housed the camera. Why did I pull that facial expression, one that inmates on death row usually pull before they meet the hooded executioner? Was I battling some angst about faith or wrestling with the internal consequences of an earlier Chicken Madras? It was not so much a pose, more a confrontation. I'm not saying that the result is ugly, but if you have problems getting your small children to go to bed at night, call me and I'll send over the photo. They'll dash under the covers at the speed of light, tearfully thankful to be away from the scary man. There isn't an airbrush powerful enough to turn this little snap into something warm and attractive. I'm expecting approaches from leading plastic surgeons, but not offering treatment. I could serve as a *before* picture in their glossy ads.

But I was unprepared for the reaction I received at passport control in London today. I was feeling relieved to actually be out of the queue, because it seemed like half the world was trying to get into the UK and there were only two border control inspectors to manage things. A kindly looking Asian man held out his hand for my passport. Bless him, he had no idea of the horror that his eyes were about to alight upon. When he flipped open my passport, and the unsmiling face of a psychopath stared back at him, he was unable to control himself. 'My God!' he exclaimed, visibly shocked. And then there was a terrible moment of embarrassment as he dug an even deeper hole: 'And you're so much younger than me too.' Then he realised he had just allowed some fairly offensive words to tumble out of his mouth. His look of horror widened. Maybe I was now a mortally offended serial killer, ageing badly, but good with an axe. Perhaps wisely, he said no more.

We often celebrate the virtue of blunt talk, and count as worthy the person who calls a spade a spade, which is good, because even in postmodernity, a spade isn't a fish. And Jesus was blunt with the religiously smug, as He sought to wake them from the cloying coma that self-righteousness brings. Paul was a straight shooter too, advising the Galatians who were bringing circumcision back into fashion to go the whole hog and just castrate themselves; not exactly comforting pastoral chat. This was blunt, and risky with it. To confront pious legalism means that the challenger always seems like a liberal rather than a freedom fighter. Grace is always most amazing (and sometimes incomprehensible) to the religious zealot.

Sometimes bluntness and thoughtlessness are married; far from being premeditated, there has been no meditation. I'm sure that the lady who strolled up to me post-sermon and asked me if I'd ever had a stroke was an innocent. I replied in the negative, silently wondered if she had any interest in surveying the surgical scars that I *do* have, and then asked her why she thought I was a stroke victim. 'It's just that, when you smile, only one side of your face goes up.' I would have smiled back at her generously, but apparently it would have been wonky.

Surely there was no malice in her question; insensitivity was her only crime. And I decided to not be offended, despite the fact that my own father had suffered a terrible stroke that stole one of his greatest joys – talking – and ultimately helped to kill him. She was not to know that. But I fear that arrogance sometimes crouches behind bluntness. So confident are we that the first notion that pops into our head must be right (or even inspired by God), we share it, uncensored by pause or reflection, and then wonder at the damage it causes. Of course, for some, that's just the point: to damage. They bully, pummel and jab with words and, when in doubt, they shout louder; victory by bluster and blasts of searing hot air. But there's nothing commendable or clever about being a verbal pit bull. Because we're good with words doesn't mean we're good.

Meanwhile, I have now arrived at my destination, and have just recovered from scaring the passport control man stiff, but have now experienced my second helping of blunt talk for the day, which is a lot to take. An unsmiling Dutch lady wandered up to me. 'We tell people straight in Holland,' she barked. 'If we think that you're ugly, we tell you you're ugly.' I braced myself. Without wanting in any way to resort to racial stereotypes, the Dutch are famous for clogs, gouda, windmills, and being devastatingly blunt.

For a moment I forgot my experience earlier in the day, back at passport control. 'Really?' I said, perplexed. 'Well, nothing like that has ever happened to me.'

Quick as a flash, and definitely not pausing for enough time to engage brain, she responded.

'Mmm. So you haven't been to Holland then …'

Or maybe she did engage brain, at the speed of light, and is very clever, and blunt with it.

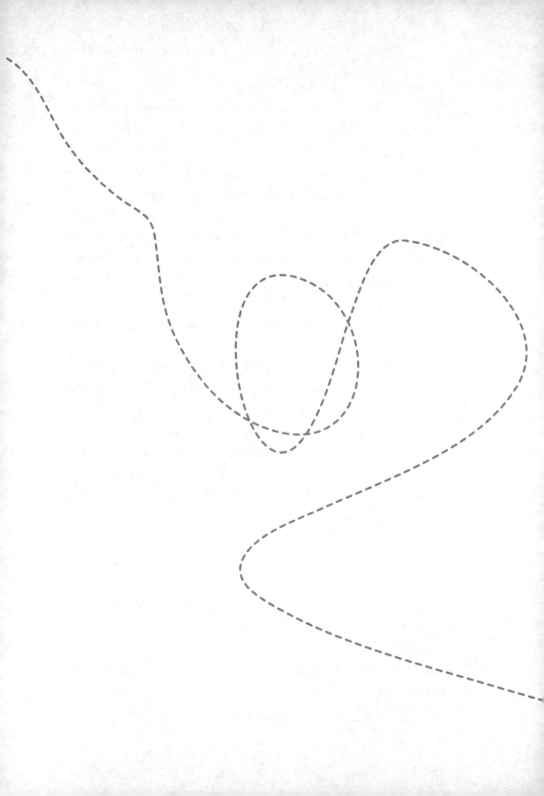

16. Healing

I believe that God still heals today. And sometimes I wish I didn't.

Before anyone rushes to gather sticks for the heretic burning, let me explain. I have to believe that healing is still a current possibility; nothing in Scripture suggests to me that the Lord has put up a 'closed' sign on the supernatural. The cessationist view that God abandoned healing and stopped giving the gifts of the Holy Spirit when the last New Testament apostle died, is frankly ludicrous and unbiblical. Over the years, I've heard of totally authenticated, stunning cases of healing that had God's fingerprints all over them. But holding out for healing can still be hard work, and not only because healing doesn't happen as often as we'd like.

First off, there's the quackery that flourishes around wholeness and sickness. Requesting prayer for a chronically ill friend recently, I received an email announcing that my ailing pal was 'HEALED in JESUS NAME!' – as if just saying it with a few *italicised CAPITAL LETTERS* and an exclamation mark(!) makes it so. How I wish it were that easy. I wanted to press reply and send 'HE ISN'T! NOW WHAT?'

Then there are those assault Christians who insist that if we just could muster up a few more mustard seeds of faith when we're sick, we'd be fixed, pronto. This sort of encouragement often leaves us feeling sicker and wondering if those so-called friends have ever been previously employed by Job, whose experience proves this sad truth: when you're in trouble, well-meaning people will show up proffering ridiculous ideas in an attempt to be helpful. Don't get really ill around these people, whatever you do. They might become jaunty about your possible imminent demise, gleefully announcing that death is just a crossing over. I'd be tempted to respond, 'Great. Sounds like a lot of fun. After you.' Or they'll tell you it's obviously your time, which might work for an octogenarian, but is hardly helpful for the dying five-year-old who has barely had a chance to do life.

Perhaps the biggest challenge when it comes to healing is that of maintaining hope, which itself can be agonising when disease continues to stalk the sufferer unchecked. I've watched helplessly when there's a refusal to concede that healing is not coming; this can rob us of the opportunity to say goodbye, and cause a person to die, not only in physical pain, but also smothered by lingering defeat, because they let the prayer team down. If there are any who should be able to stare death down, it's the followers of the resurrected Jesus. And I'm heartbroken at the lack of farewells; if I were going on a lengthy journey or emigrating to the other side of the earth, I'd want the opportunity to gather family and friends to bid them farewell. How many Christians have been robbed of that most vital goodbye, because they felt that conceding that death was imminent was tantamount to a failure?

But there was a time recently when I definitely *was* glad to believe in healing, mainly because I desperately needed some. I was sick, and the doctor was looking worried, which was worrying. I absentmindedly began counting the furrows on his brow. There were five, and there was no sign of them smoothing out. The treatment that he'd prescribed wasn't working and, for a while, the prognosis wasn't great, if dying can be described as not being great.

It all began in a London restaurant. Swine flu was not actually listed on the menu, but halfway through the meal I caught it and suddenly decided to never eat food again. Within days the flu morphed to double pneumonia, and I wasn't getting better.

Ordered to have a CT scan, fear mugged me, brutally. I was convinced that a sinister cancer was lurking somewhere deep in my lungs, and that my days were very numbered. And here is my real disappointment: I wish I could write that I felt a surge of faith for this trying season, that God's presence overwhelmed me and sent terror packing, that I had to be forcibly restrained from taking my tambourine into the scanner, so determined was I to be a faithful worshipper.

Instead, I emerged from that humming tube, flushed warm from the liquid they had pumped through my veins, and collapsed into my wife's arms, sobbing like a baby. Scratch that. Even babies don't howl that loud. I was weak and utterly pathetic. Send me a badge with the word 'wimp' on it. My confidence crumbled like a sandcastle in the wake of a fast tide. I so wanted to be brave, a warrior, like Russell Crowe. Instead I turned into Frank Spencer, my wife an unwitting Betty. I am embarrassed even as I remember it.

And of this I was sure: I certainly did not want to die. I greatly admire those Christians who seem able to look at breathing their last with, well, breathless anticipation. Do I want to see Jesus, or perhaps bump into the apostle Paul and ask him whether he ever got his cloak back? Certainly I do. But not just now, thank you very much.

There was no cancer, there was no supernatural healing, but my lungs finally cleared, and, as you've probably noticed, at the time of publication at least, I'm not dead. But the experience has left me with a tiny understanding of what illness feels like. I was grateful for the assurance of caring prayers. And the present suffering of very dear friends makes me desperate to see some healing action.

So I don't want the quackery that flourishes in the smog that illness creates. And I want to be able to bid a dying someone farewell, without feeling the shame of the vanquished. But I continue to believe that God still heals today. Sometimes I wish I didn't. And mostly I'm glad I do.

17. Peeled potatoes

For some reason, he wouldn't eat baked potatoes with the skins left on. He always insisted that they were peeled. I thought he was just being picky, which he most certainly was not.

My soldier father was captured during the Second World War, and spent three years behind the barbed wire of Italian and German prison camps. It must have been terrifying for a nineteen-year-old, barely graduated from adolescence, to find himself as a captive, destined to surrender his early twenties to incarceration, near starvation and endless uncertainty. Like most of his generation, he never spoke much about those days; 'Keep calm and carry on' is more than a slogan that's become fashionable again, emblazoned on mugs and tea towels; it was the way a people at war did life. Steady as you go. Don't make a fuss.

All I knew was that he escaped during a six-week final death march, as the Germans frantically fled from the advancing Russian army, herding their prisoners as they did. With shining eyes he spoke of the moment of decision when he chose a dangerous dash to freedom. Capture meant certain death. A bend in the road offered a ten second window when he was out of sight and shot of the trigger-happy guards; he and a friend staggered into the woods, filthy, starving fugitives.

At last they stumbled upon a house and found a German woman

and her young family there; she was terrified of these emaciated, flea-bitten POWs, fearing rape, violence or worse. Assuring her that they meant her no harm, they asked only for a place to sleep the night, and a meal of potatoes. Peeled potatoes, if you please. They must be peeled.

And that was all he told me about those dark days.

As a teenager, I became a Christian, and he was appalled. He snorted in disbelief when I told him, loudly, of my encounter with the God of love. But he only protested once. With the dogged fervency peculiar to the zealous convert, I harassed him and cajoled him and insisted that he repent. When he briefly mentioned the subject of suffering, I quoted scripture after scripture like a quick-draw gunfighter. I prodded and jabbed at him with my clever, small, so-called answers, and assumed that he just had a hard, rebellious heart. I was wrong again. I often am.

Unsurprisingly, he didn't respond to my gospel haranguing by becoming a keen convert. Two decades later – by which time I'd learned to shut up – he finally became a follower of Jesus himself, and then died shortly after, some seventeen years ago now.

Pondering his life, there have been times when I have wondered about his three lost years in the camps. What were his days like? Who were his friends? How did they stay hopeful and not lose their minds?

And then, last week, I stumbled upon a secret treasure that broke my heart and challenged my soul. Flipping through an old document box, I discovered the letter that the Red Cross sent to my grandparents when my father was captured. It was good news and bad news; good, in that he had been missing in action for six months. Now, after a harrowing half a year when they feared that their son was a shattered corpse somewhere in the North African desert, they knew he was alive. But the bad news was that he was a prisoner of war. The letter named the last prison camp he was in.

How the world has changed. A decade ago, to find out more about those lost years of my father's life, I would have needed to travel to his regimental headquarters, in search of browning, faded documents. Perhaps I might have needed to travel to Germany or Italy, accompanied by a translator, to scour libraries and visit wartime locations. But now all that has changed, because of the internet. Previously elusive information is now just a few key strokes away. Not expecting much, I tapped the name of the *stalag* into Google, and within seconds my father's world exploded in front of me. I was unprepared for what I found.

The camp where he was held was just five miles from Auschwitz, and was worse than I ever imagined. The captives were kept on a starvation diet in barracks that were infested with fleas. I saw photographs of some prisoners with thick chains around the necks, which the guards would twist, tighter and tighter, just for fun. Some were shot in the head for not working hard enough, dispatched at a cruel whim. I discovered that the final march was a freezing hell. In Germany's coldest winter in a hundred years, a bone-weary train of thousands trudged their way across 600 miles of frozen road; a swift jab with a rifle butt to the back of the neck ended the life of any who stumbled, left to die in a roadside ditch, that terrible roadway was littered with frozen corpses.

I wept as I remembered my clever little 'answers' on the subject of suffering, but also his quiet smile as I parroted them in his face. How easily he could have shattered my boldness with just one story of his pain, but he never did. He held a trump card that could have won any exchange, but he chose to never play it. I always thought that I was trying to show him what grace was when, all along, his silence in the face of my naive brashness was the real triumph of grace. If only I had known his story.

Every person has a story. Their reactions are the product of their journey: encouragements, rejections, triumphs and failures, joys and pains, exhilaration and devastation. Everyone is a living library, a catalogue of episodes; remembering that might cause us to hesitate and think before we bluster or judge. We are all products of our past.

I also learned about the starvation diet that the prisoners endured. For breakfast, they were given nothing. In the evening, a small cube of hard black bread. And at midday, thin watery soup, void of protein, and three tiny potatoes, which were usually green and rotten.

And always served with the skins left on.

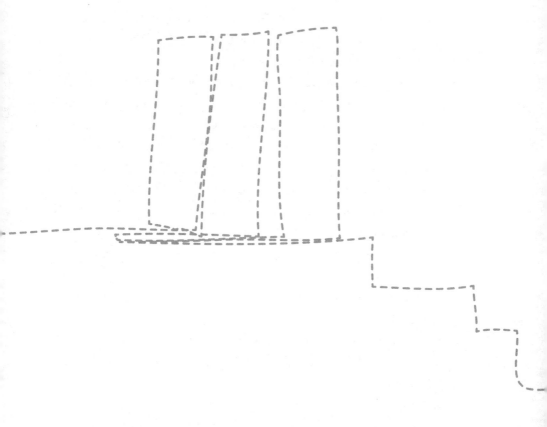

18. Preaching

Preaching is an amazing privilege, but it can be perilous too, especially in the main danger zone: the period immediately after the Sunday morning service. People are either darting for the door in search of dead chicken and gravy, or perhaps standing around sipping weak tea while wishing that their biscuits were chocolate covered. It's then that the thoughtless, the hapless and the sometimes downright carnivorous commentators occasionally descend on the preacher.

There are those who march up to the preacher with a 'deep' question to ask, but it soon becomes obvious that they already know the answer – they just want to know if the preacher does. Theirs is not an enquiry, it's a test, and one that I often fail. Triumphant, they walk away, apparently thrilled to have discovered a gap in my knowledge bank.

Sadly, occasionally preachers bump into thoroughly nasty people who make Simon Cowell look shy, and are pious with it. 'That was the biggest load of rubbish I've ever heard in my life. God bless you!' said one chap as he shook my hand at speed in his vice-like grip, while grinning broadly in a style reminiscent of Hannibal Lecter. Perhaps he thought that the afterthought of blessing might soften the blow of the curse that preceded it. He thought wrong.

Preaching provides plenty of fuel for complaining. I've received angry letters because I didn't maintain enough eye contact with every section of the congregation; I try to scan the crowd, but it can give the impression that I am high on something. I upset one gentleman (whose impossibly hairy nostrils really upset me, as he snorted through what looked like Sherwood Forest) because I slightly mispronounced a Hebrew word. And the version of the Bible that the preacher uses can ignite dismay. Some people sniff if you use the *Good News* or *Message* versions. And as an NIV devotee, I chirpily suggested that those who used the *Amplified Version* could finish off the reading after lunch. Imagine the letter:

'Dear Jeff, I was upset *(offended, dismayed, affronted, incensed)* by your attitude towards the *Amplified Version* today ...'

Then there are those who get upset for no reason I can think of. 'I am rather disgusted that the speaker tonight said that the name of God is not mentioned in the book of Esther' said one growling complainant. 'What do you have to say to that, eh?'

'Well. I suppose I'd have to say that there's no mention of the name of God in the book of Esther,' I replied, which didn't seem to help him. He marched off, apparently in search of someone who would sympathise with his disappointment, not so much with the speaker, but with the author of Esther. But still the speaker – and perhaps I – got the blame.

Of course there are many moments of encouragement for the preacher, but even some of these can be a little strange. I'm never sure how to respond to the person who thanks me profusely for what I said about a particular issue, which is nice, except when I didn't get within a hundred miles of that subject.

And then there are the times when someone hears something that is not only not what the preacher is saying, but is the precise opposite to it. I have frequently spoken about how the architects of South African apartheid used Bible verses to construct their oppressive doctrine.

Members of our church, themselves South Africans, introduced themselves during a 'turn around and say hello' moment in one of our services. They were greeted with a stunningly offensive statement: 'Oh, you're from South Africa, are you? Jeff is always telling us about just how bad South Africans are.' Not exactly a welcoming, heart-warming moment. Of course for me to suggest that South Africans are bad would make me guilty of exactly the same brand of racist stereotyping that I was vehemently condemning. And I've spoken up against the British Victorians using Scripture to justify hanging children for stealing a loaf of bread (which doesn't make all Brits bad), and against the racism of sixties America, where black people were forced to sit at the back of the bus, and were made to frequent different bathrooms from white people, until Martin Luther King and others began to speak up. And none of this means that Americans are bad: just that all humans are fallen, and fallen people create warped and fallen ideologies. However, all of this was lost on my hearer – and we could have alienated a couple of lovely South Africans as a result. What is heard is not always what was said.

I am aware that preachers themselves are far from perfect. I've frequently been guilty of engaging mouth before brain, yelling for no reason, and having strange habits that can be disconcerting. My glasses tend to slip down my nose while I'm speaking, which is awkward when I have a microphone in one hand and a Bible in the other. My solution is to suddenly throw my head back, hoping that my glasses will flip up and land back home on the bridge of my nose. This violent head jerking creates quite a stir in the congregation. Some worry that I am having a fit, and wonder if members of St John Ambulance should be summoned. Other more enthusiastically charismatic types conclude that I'm having an involuntary Holy Spirit manifestation, shout 'More Lord!!' and do a spot of head jerking themselves.

But despite our foibles, spare a prayer and a kind word for the preachers in your life: they are women and men who need encouragement, even if some try to resist it, like one minister who was irrationally paranoid about praise and struggled when one of his congregation tried to express gratitude for the sermon. 'No!' cried the frantic preacher, desperate to ensure that credit was only given where credit was due. 'No, madam, don't thank me, it was the Lord.'

'Well, actually, it wasn't that good,' she responded. Mmm. Serves him right.

19. Encounter

Once upon a time nearly half a century ago, five lads grew up in neighbouring streets in London. More Essex boys than junior Eastenders, they journeyed together from short trousers at the infant's school, through to the pubescent awkwardness of secondary modern. They shared the same classrooms, love of Led Zeppelin, hairstyles and even went out with the same girls, though not usually at the same time. They argued, made up, drank beer and spent a thousand Saturdays kicking a football around the park. They sat around and looked up at the stars and wondered if anything meant anything.

Like most youthful friends, they always planned to be friends for life, but school-leaving changed all that. They scattered in different directions to trek down different career paths: one, a recording engineer; another, a vice principal of a college. There was a BBC producer and a health and safety inspector. And a minister of religion.

My drifting from the group was accelerated by my teenage conversion, throwing myself into church activities and then heading off to college for ministry training. The little band of pals lost touch for thirty-five years – until last night, when Phil, Graham, Trevor, Steve and I met once more. It was nothing short of wonderful.

Finding one another through the mixed blessing that is social networking, we scheduled our reunion in a London pub. I'd been looking forward to the meeting for months. Now, as I gingerly opened the door and peered around the crowded bar, looking for a group of seventeen-year-old chaps turned fifty-two, anxiety momentarily mugged me. And then I was greeted by four broad, welcoming smiles. Recognising the group, even after all those years, was easy. But there was to be one surprise encounter that I hadn't reckoned on.

Within seconds we were laughing out loud at the memory of some of our teachers. There was strange Mr Foot (chemistry), who lectured us endlessly about laboratory safety, which was ironic, seeing as he looked as if half his head had been blown away by a mishap with a Bunsen burner. We remembered Mr Peckett (French), a staunch disciplinarian whose terrible breath could have controlled rioting crowds, and who spanked us by karate chopping our buttocks, which we didn't think was too strange back then, but reflection made us wonder ... We smiled wistfully at the mention of the gorgeous drama teacher; her name escaped us, but we remembered her miniskirt very well ...

Delighted to be together, we solemnly vowed, not only to attend each others' funerals, but to ensure that a death would not be the prompt for the next reunion, arranging to meet again in just two months. The evening was marked with great kindness and respect. I knew that I had been a little too fervent as a new Christian, and was concerned that they might view me as a friend turned religious fanatic. I needn't have worried.

'You had a life altering experience when you were seventeen, Jeff,' said Phil. 'Please tell us about it.' I did, and they were kind enough to listen. As I recounted my story, I nervously glanced around the table, to spot rolled eyes of mockery or shared glances of boredom. I needn't have worried.

But then came the encounter that I hadn't expected, as a person I barely recognised suddenly showed up. That someone was me, as I used to be. 'We were amazed when you got God,' smiled Trevor, 'because you were always the bad lad of the group.' I learned that they'd started smoking because I, sadly, had led the way. They said that I was brave (which I think means stupid) because I took risks and then they'd have to follow. I listened wide-eyed as they told me their perceptions of my home and my upbringing. I'd always felt a little like an outsider; now I realised that my acts of bravado might have been about needing to prove myself, and I wondered how much this little boy had grown up. The cigarettes are long gone, but the need for approval persistently lingers.

At last the evening finished with hugs goodbye, and I boarded the train, thrilled to have reconnected with them, and intrigued to have gained their insights about me.

Surely that's what veteran friendships can be – a mirror kindly held up before us, showing us what we cannot see in ourselves. Friends can show us our blind spots, our foibles, our strengths and our screamingly irritating habits, if we will let them. If we scatter eggshells around us, insist that anyone who gets close to us will have to walk on them and demand that they read an autocue that will flatter us, then we won't ever benefit from their insights. Perhaps our friends have some things that they're desperate to tell us, if only we would ask.

Friends – they can introduce us to people that we've lost touch with for a while. Like ourselves.

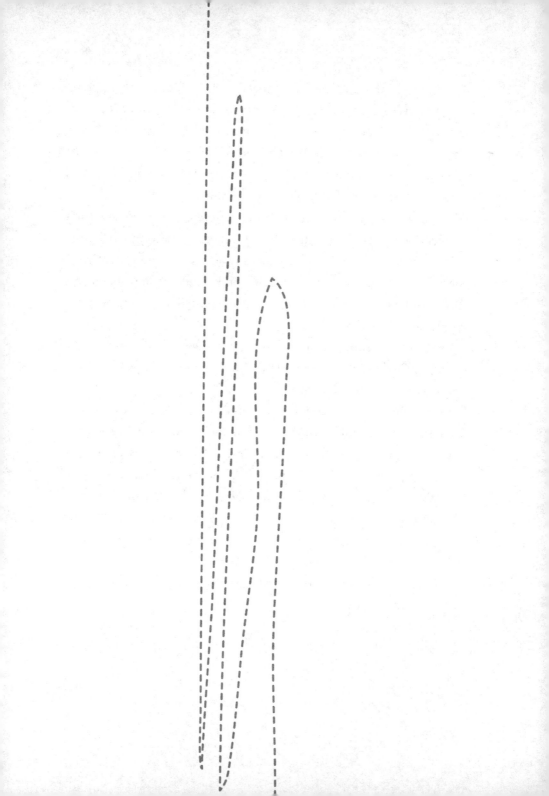

20. The gladiatorial guard

It made a refreshing change from the computerised announcements that are broadcast on trains and stations these days: 'The Eastbourne train is delayed by ten minutes, I am very sorry for any inconvenience this causes to your journey.' Right. Sincerity is suspect in a robotic pre-recorded announcement, so the sorrow sounds like a sham. When a computer is 'sorry', does it pause for a moment of grief, locking its own keyboard out of respect, but when it's 'very sorry', does it self-destruct it's own hard drive? Mechanised sorrow is unconvincing.

So there I was, parked in front of my computer on yet another train, and the very live and spontaneous announcement that the guard made was surprising and refreshing.

'Ladies and gentlemen, this is your guard speaking. This train is delayed. I've got no idea why. I could make up an excuse for you, but I won't bother. It's just delayed, and that's that. I'll let you know if I find out any more news. In the meantime, I'm really sorry.'

I smiled at his uncluttered candour, but then, just a minute later, the train PA crackled again. This time it was the driver, who was obviously miffed at his colleague's frankness. He blew into the microphone, like an amateur Elvis impersonator taking to the stage, and spoke with the odd staccato of a Northern club singer.

'A–ladies and a–gentlemen, this is your driver speaking–er, and following the er–recent announcement made by my colleague, who is a–usually very professional, allow me–er to provide you with the er–reasons for the delay to this service.'

He then gave a lengthy explanation for the tardiness, and said he was sure that his highly experienced guard (who was also a long-serving staff member) would respond helpfully to any further enquiries about the service. The tension between them was palpable; these chaps were having a very public spat over the PA. Incredibly, within seconds the guard came back on to make a further response. This train journey was getting interesting, and could possibly lead to a world war.

'Ladies and gentlemen, this is your guard here. My colleague, the driver, is quite right, and I am delighted to confirm that this train will arrive at its various destinations ... eventually.'

I laughed out loud, and most of the carriage joined me, but then I realised that I had just witnessed an escalation of conflict. Instead of having a quiet word in private about appropriate procedures and announcement protocol, these two railroad gladiators were taking their irritations with each other out into a very public arena.

Watching others quarrelling is always uncomfortable; I've experienced a few buttock-crunching moments when married couples have sniped at each other in front of me during a shared meal, or during a car journey. Awkwardness shrouds what moments earlier was a happy event; I find myself staring woodenly at my food as if utterly fascinated by it, or out of the window studying a perfectly ordinary tree, hoping and praying that they'll call time on their squabble. And it's even worse if they try to draw me in and take sides. What do *you* think, Jeff? I think you should wait until you're alone, and I'm out of earshot, and then you can sort yourselves out, that's what I think.

Sometimes churches are shattered because we turn personal conflicts into church-wide feuds.

There's plenty to get upset about in church, be it our pew preference, the woman with the spaceship-sized hat which eclipses the sun, the vicar's pompous preaching voice or that irritating person with whom we simply have a personality clash. We turn small grievances into public vendettas, drag other people into the ring and end up with an unseemly congregational fist fight. Groups form into indignant, self-righteous gangs, who want to score points and win rather than resolve the issue peaceably before long, seismic cracks appear, and churches fracture and divide, sometimes irreparably. People become vicariously offended for each other, the original contentious issue fades into insignificance and the fight itself becomes the focus, which makes resolution difficult, if not impossible. Anger is not a laser-directed missile that zeros in on one target, but a bomb that can create collateral havoc everywhere. I've seen the carnage too often.

So when we're irritated in our friendships, marriages or churches (and when it comes to church, if we've been part of one for more than six months, and nothing has upset us yet, we're probably clinically dead), before we reach for the proverbial microphone, let's pause. Perhaps this can all be sorted out quietly, without a public spat.

And although it might take great grace, epic patience and a willingness to forgive for the seventieth time, perhaps we will arrive at a beautiful destination, a place of peace and reconciliation. Although, as the guard cheerfully reminded us, these things might take time, but we might get there.

Eventually.

21. Bored

Surely it's due to the advent of a gazillion television channels. Desperate to find something interesting to point their cameras at, production companies are now serving up large helpings of viewing slop. Channel surfing today, I was treated to a half-hour programme (on BBC1, not an obscure satellite channel with an audience of nine) where a contest, complete with simulated drum rolls, was staged between a celebrity chef and a fish and chip shop, to see who could fry the best battered cod. The 'climax' of this blockbuster was when a blindfolded couple from somewhere north of Watford tasted the combination of cod, chips and mushy peas, and declared the Italian chef to be the winner. Be still my beating heart. The BBC's mission has always been to educate …

And then there's that show where morally outraged cleaning ladies go into scruffy (and sometimes filthy) homes of people who are, in some cases, so crusty that the turbo-cleaners might do better to stop by their homes with a wrecking ball, or use them as a bio-chemical threat against Iran. In this gripping piece of telly, those found with fat stains behind their cookers are treated with the disdain normally shown to drug cartel barons. Yawn.

These shows are only slightly more interesting than that numbing encounter with Ant, Dec and a gaggle of former celebrities faffing around in a jungle eating eels and scorpions. Please. I'm a licence payer. Get me out of here.

All this numbing stuff brings me to the conclusion that (a) anyone who regularly watches television, especially daytime television, is likely to lose their mind and (b) boredom is one of the great Satans destroying our culture from within, like a bug gnawing away at the innards of an apple. We're slowly being bored senseless, which will ultimately lead to our being bored to death.

Technology should have made us hyper, the most stimulated culture ever. We have the ability to download limitless information on our smartphones, save planet Earth from dark marauders through our X-boxes, watch Buzz Lightyear in 3D, and be guitar heroes or fitness freaks with our Wii's (for those blessed to be techno-ignorant, a Wii is a Nintendo game console, not a urine infection). And yet we're bored.

Marriages disintegrate, because we're bored with talking to or sleeping with the same person. Young people aspire to being famous for nothing in particular, because even the brightest job looks dull. A good night out on the town with friends is no longer satisfactory, as binge drinkers summarily descend into senselessness and, just a few hours later in the morning, can't even remember the people they were with, or the exploits they performed.

Some churches are being vacated, not because people are abandoning God, but rather are looking for Him, and have given up hope of finding Him in what have become temples of the tedious. The exodus from church happens, not necessarily because of doctrine, but dullness.

Boredom is a three-piece-suited killer dressed in inconspicuous grey. Bored, we tumble down slippery steps of madness in order to escape the dreary, if only for a while. Apathetic, neutralised souls, we would rise up and cry in unison, 'Are we bovvered?' if only we could be bothered.

And so I'd like to propose a two-part strategy in order to deal with boredom: let's make friends with it, and declare war on it. Let's make our peace with tedium, accepting that every day is not going to be loaded with adrenaline-fuelled adventure. Let's be real about our marriages and churches: sometimes we carry on, not because everything is fantastic or exhilarating, but because we're called to faithfulness. Be committed to your church, not to how high you jumped last Sunday. Don't join the mobile crowd who dash from church to church on blessing/excitement safari.

But at the same time, let's battle what has become tiresome and predictable. That's not a call to our churches to become slaves to endless innovation, or confuse tradition with traditionalism. But let's literally play at church, as we experiment, create and innovate.

And let's know that, in our personal lives, a walk on the wilder side won't demand huge, expensive choices. Take a walk in the sea – with your clothes on. Picnic in a park during a rainstorm. Make love where you usually make tea. Be smart, and turn your smartphone off for a day once a week. Listen rather than talk. Invite that neighbour in for a coffee. Discover a new author. Write a letter to the paper.

Meanwhile, I've come up with a great idea to improve what's on the telly. Why not put a bunch of pleasant but unspectacular folks in a house for a few weeks and do nothing other than watch them? We could see them argue, canoodle in a hot tub, even sleep. Then they could emerge and live scandalously, and produce fuel for the Sunday tabloids.

Ooops, sorry. That's been done. *Boring.*

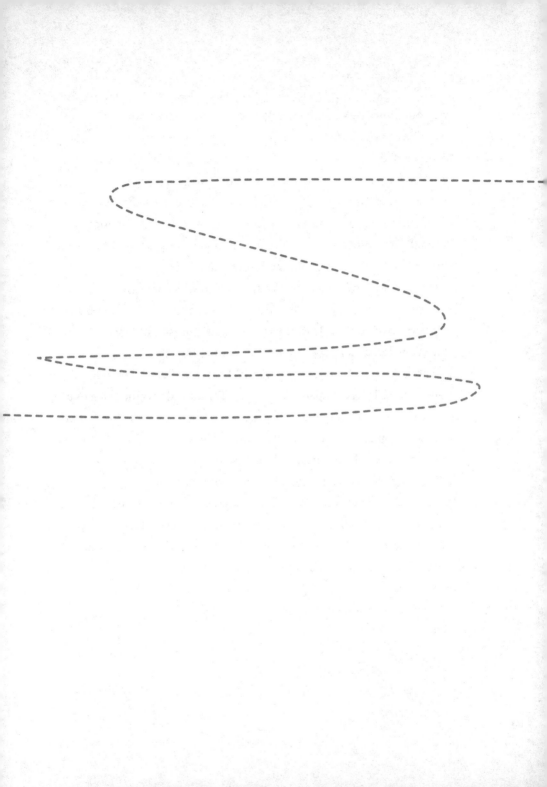

22. Arm wrestling

As soon as I set eyes on him, I knew he was trouble. He stomped down the aisle towards me, boarding pass clenched in his fist, an angry scowl occupying his whole face. I hoped he wouldn't be sitting anywhere near me, in vain. He snapped open the overhead compartment, tut-tutted because other passengers had also felt the need to store their bags up there, and shoved his briefcase in with attitude.

He was sitting in the window seat, next to me. 'Excuse me,' he hissed, stepping over my legs without waiting for me to move them, providing a souvenir of our encounter in the form of a bruise. No apology was offered, and even though we'd only been vaguely acquainted for thirty seconds, no apology was anticipated. And then the extended tirade began, my fellow passenger's war with the world. He punched the call button with attitude, which summoned the flight attendant with its ping, and berated her for the late departure; apparently she was responsible for the planet's weather systems. She really must do better.

Ping. His headset didn't work properly, meaning he was unable to watch the movie. Ping. The coffee was too strong, bring me another one, and make it fresh. Ping. He demanded two meals instead of one, and was outraged when he was denied. Ping. Ping. Now he was bleating loudly. 'Ever since I've been on this flight, I've not been treated well.'

Poor lamb. I was beginning to think that this little lamb needed to pay a visit to the slaughterhouse.

He was so consistently rude and demanding that a flight attendant quietly offered to move me to another seat. Mercifully, he took a short nap, and I looked over at his face. His brow was furrowed deep, ploughed by his constant frown. He tossed around restlessly, murmuring and then snorting. He was sleeping, but was unable to rest. I wondered if he was ranting in dreamland.

I wish that I could report that I nudged him from his fitful slumber and told him about the peace and love that Jesus offers, whereupon he wept like a baby, apologised for being angry since being prenatal, handed the flight crew wedges of cash as an act of contrition, and asked if there was an onboard Alpha course available. Instead, I just sat there, fantasising about ejector seats, which would be activated by his pressing the call button. Ping. *Whoosh.*

And then I silently embarked on the battle for the armrest. He had spread himself out, his right arm covering and indeed overflowing the armrest that was supposed to be shared between us. Now I understand how real wars start. It's all about territory. I was quietly outraged at the invasion of my space, so I plotted a takeover. He yawned, holding his arms up in the air for a moment, so I took the opportunity to slip my arm onto the thin strip of leatherette covered metal that separated us. His arm fell back down onto my forearm. Now we looked like an unhappy couple. I conceded defeat, and gently extracted my arm.

His ire outlasted the flight; later I would see him in the airport, remonstrating with yet another airline employee, his arms flailing like a windmill, his face flushed dangerously crimson, the hapless employee flinching, bowed by his furious blast.

And so I began to speculate. He is a man on a lifelong mission. He is permanently looking for trouble, and hunting for an opportunity to be offended. Perhaps he has gone through life feeling like a victim, with a vague sense that circumstances and people are quietly conspiring against him. And I've met a few Christians just like him. Grace has enabled them to escape wrath, but wrath is what they pass around. They can make church life a nightmare. They are never happy. If the very dead were raised on Sunday morning, it's possible that they'd be upset, because the service was delayed while they disposed of the coffins. The church building is too hot, or too cold. They love the drums/hate the drums/wonder loudly if the drums are biblical. They are the faithful fumers, and the sound of crunched eggshells can be deafening when others try to get close to them. Paranoia prods them to resist change, feeling it to be a personal affront, especially if their preferences are being violated. They park themselves on the precipice of rage and are nudged into yet another outburst by the smallest thing.

They are rarely confronted. People usually try to appease those who are serially irritated. They are tagged as 'difficult' or 'sensitive', and most do their best to avoid them.

Sometimes they start a club, an informal gathering of the disaffected, with devastating effects. And the sad truth is this: we can all so easily be like this, as I was about to discover.

Mr Angry started to snore. And as I sat there, bristling at his grunting and stunned by the tragic injustice of not being able to use the armrest, I realised that my brow was furrowed too.

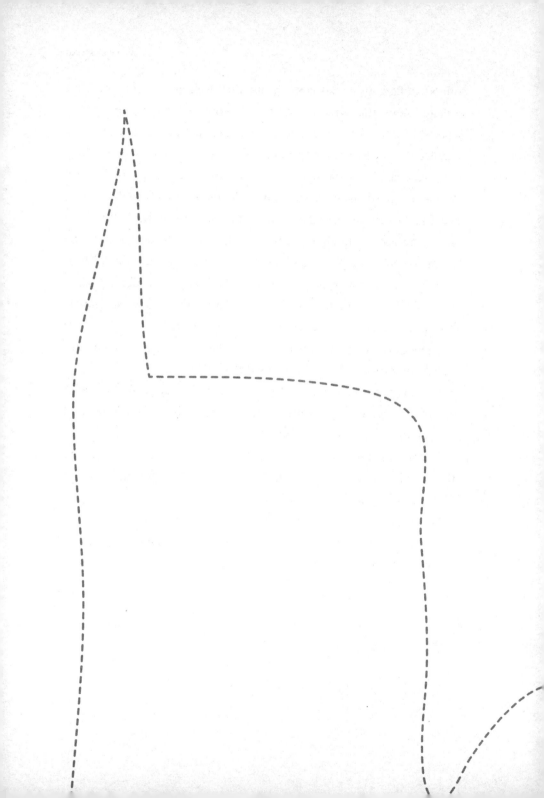

23. The first day

My first day as a Bible college student was absolutely terrifying. As we gathered for our first chapel, I glanced around at the gaggle of rather keen looking Christians, and immediately felt like an imposter. They all looked so breathless and certain, and had probably sung hymns as they drove to the college; some, I thought, were likely to have been cautioned by the local constabulary for raising their hands worshipfully while driving. One or two had that faraway look that suggested that they were somehow already camped out on heaven's shores, and were just navigating through earth as day trippers.

We were a mixed bunch. Among our number there were some sweet, smiling church girls, all giggles and innocence, a bemused retired policeman, an Orangeman from Belfast who was hilarious and angry in turn, and an impossibly hairy Iranian. And it was rumoured that one of the new students had formerly been a Triad gang member in the walled city of Hong Kong. A kung fu expert, apparently he could kill with just the flick of an eyelid. I decided, notwithstanding his conversion, to call him 'Sir'. Better safe than sorry.

We all shared two things in common. We were awash with hope and optimism, and it seemed we were all available to God's purposes for our lives, although this created some struggles. One hapless chap fretted endlessly that God might call him to be a missionary in some far-flung foreign clime. He had obviously been taught the warped notion that God's will for our lives is usually the exact opposite of what we'd naturally like to do, which is a very weird way to look at life. This apparently means that to fulfil the will of God for my life, I need to become a bungee jumper (I hate the thought), go on holiday to Clacton-on-Sea (no offence, but I did more than my fair share of Clacton days out as a child) and live on a diet of Ethiopian food (it's the only exotic cuisine that I seriously dislike).

Our friend obviously loathed the idea of missions work and hated hot weather, hence his terror that God had a nasty trick calling up His sleeve. And so as an act of revenge for his buffalo-like snoring, a few students gathered around his bed while he was loudly sleeping, and whispered the phrase, 'Go to India' about 300 times. The next morning he sat bolt upright in bed, sheer panic masking his face. 'Last night I heard so many voices commanding me to go overseas,' he whimpered, much to the delight of the whispering team. Later in the day we heard he was marching around the college car park, praying in tongues and telling God he was willing to go, even if this included embracing a curry centred diet. Naughtily, another student and I climbed up onto the college roof and wailed the plaintive call, 'Come to India!' in an eerie voice. He looked heavenward, abject terror masking his face.

Our first lecture sobered us up. The session opened with a welcome, and then words I'll never forget: 'Ten years from now, many of you won't be following Jesus.' The warning was like a stun grenade. Most of us looked around the room, wondering who the future deserters might be, the Judases in our midst. A few rolled their eyes in disdain, dismissing the lecturer as an out-of-touch, stuffy academic, who didn't know anything about the real world, as if we did. Some wondered if he was joking, engaging in dark humour to get our attention. But the gloomy ten-year prophecy was to be fulfilled.

Some entered full-time ministry, and dropped out almost immediately, which for most was no failure, but realignment. But some drifted away from faith. One was to serve a lengthy prison sentence. Two of our number took their own lives. Marriages crumbled. The survival rate was not high.

There *were* those who stood out because of the beautiful simplicity of their faith, like Joy, a pretty, vivacious blond who had a personality that embodied her name. Prior to college, she had served as a missionary nurse, but she never once played the 'I've got ministry experience' card. She returned to Zimbabwe after graduating, and died too young. While assisting in a makeshift operating theatre, she was infected with blood contaminated by the AIDS virus. She gave her life in service of the people she loved.

And some remain in Christian faith and service today in a wide variety of spheres.

But as we gathered for that first lecture, there are some things that I wish I'd known.

I wish we'd all understood that the Christian life is often an uphill trek, and not a downhill skip. That haunting questions and debilitating doubts will cast shadows over the journey. I wish we'd known that weirdness doesn't equal spirituality. One or two of our intake were misdiagnosed as being deeply spiritual, when I'm now convinced that they were actually suffering from mental illnesses with religious symptoms. There was the chap who prayed for hours, talking not only to God, but chatting with the flowers too; we thought he was deeply religious, but I think he was actually ill, and needed help.

And I wish I'd known that study was vital. I wasted so much time at college, fooled by youthful arrogance into thinking that academia didn't matter, that only anointing did. I spent too much time messing around, like the night we scared the reluctant missionary when we climbed up onto the roof.

But something great came out of that. That chap is still out in India, where he has served for thirty years as a result of the 'call' we gave him.

No, he's not. I'm joking.

But the Old Testament professor with the prophetic warning was not joking. Let's stay hopeful, available – and faithful. To the last breath, or until He comes.

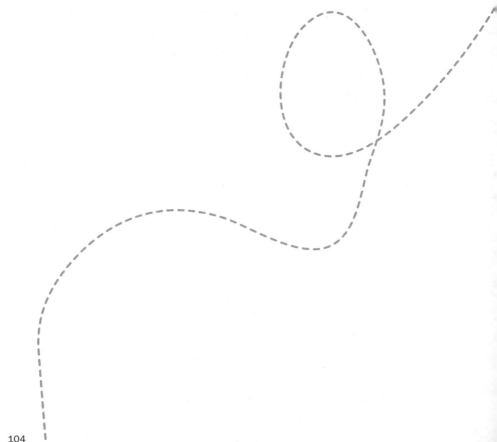

24. Hello, Jumbo

Years ago, I was considering a pastoral post in an American church, and hopped over the pond to discuss it. A British friend accompanied me. Looking back, I'm grateful to have had a friend at my side. We were to navigate a terrifying skirmish together and needed each other for support.

The first sign of challenge came when we discovered we were not staying at a local hotel. A lady from the church had offered hospitality, but her husband was out of town, which felt awkward, and things got even more worrying when we arrived at her home. She welcomed us with a hug and then announced that she'd invited a young lady from the church to join us for dinner. This was starting to feel like a rather uncomfortable foursome. I considered protesting, but it would have sounded rude, ungrateful. Besides, I decided, nothing could possibly go wrong, surely, because my friend and I could watch each others' backs. How naive I was. I was quite unprepared for what would unfold during the evening. If you are of sensitive disposition, then turn to the next piece. What follows is stark and ugly.

We sat down for an excellent meal, helpfully sprinkled with intensely religious conversation. All talk was of answered prayers, sublime worship experiences and the meaning of various obscure Bible verses.

Then we turned to discuss the church, what God was doing, what He was saying. I started to relax: the possibility of us being morally compromised seemed remote. And indeed, we *were* perfectly safe. The challenge was to come from another surprising turn in the evening.

During dessert, the young lady guest excused herself from the table, and stepped into the loo which, unhappily, was sited just off the dining room. Within seconds, as we three remaining diners continued our religious conversation, I became very frightened. From the extremely loud explosions that emanated from the loo, it seemed that a reenactment of the Battle of Britain, or something equally epic, was happening in there. I'm sorry to be so graphic (I did forewarn you), but some remarkable sounds made up the symphonic cacophony that echoed from that small room. When the lady returned to the table minutes later heartily relieved, we were relieved too – that she had survived. I didn't know whether to enquire about her health, ask if she needed a paramedic or recommend she join a brass band. But we were not done. Five minutes later, she excused herself once more and repeated the performance, and we hadn't even clapped for an encore. And we three just carried on chatting, as if nothing untoward was happening, even though we actually had to raise our voices a little to be heard over the not-too-distant sounds of battle. I concentrated on not catching my friend's eye, focusing on thoughts of death, and pinching my thighs under the table to prevent a total collapse into gales of laughter. When the young lady finally returned from a second performance that was reminiscent of the 1812 Overture, we continued our conversation about the authorship of Ecclesiastes. There was an elephant in the room (and possibly another one in the bathroom), but we all politely disregarded it and carried on regardless.

Elephant avoidance often happens in the church. Painfully aware of tension, disagreement and sometimes downright hostility, we avoid acknowledging the presence of the proverbial big ears because we can't bear the thought of conflict. And so we fake love, fabricate fellowship, resort to blathering small talk, but can't escape the agitation that is natural when we know that big issues are deliberately being ignored. We hesitate to mention what feels unmentionable. Sometimes church leaders create a culture of subservience where there are so many unacknowledged elephants around, everyone lives under the threat of a stampede. We're made to feel nervous to raise an eyebrow, never mind a question. Dissent is a dirty word in those churches, and we nod our heads in agonised compliancy even though we're convinced that something is very wrong. Churches high on vision have a tendency towards this: so convinced are they that they are on a mission from God that voices of dissent are not only ignored, but are dismissed as being divisive, and there's a threat of a witch burning. We're intimidated into smiling silence.

But unacknowledged elephants don't sit quietly and harmlessly in the corner. Ignoring them doesn't tame them – on the contrary, they'll stamp around and create havoc. Silenced people eventually lose hope and heart, and drift away from church, still unable to acknowledge why they went.

Not everything needs sorting out; let's not major on minors, or turn mice into giants. I don't want to be a Christian on endless safari, always on the hunt for issues to raise and complaints to make. But if, in your church, there's a large grey chap with a trunk who answers to the name of Jumbo, it might be time to acknowledge that he's actually in the room.

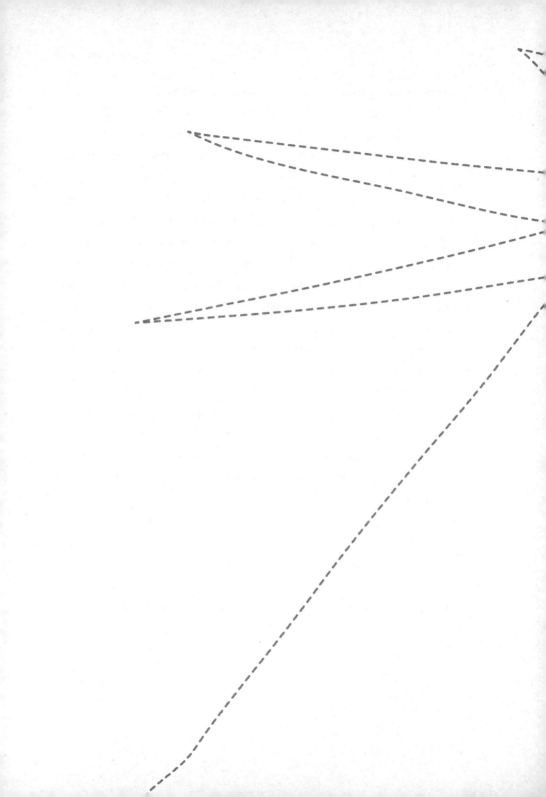

25. Epic?

It was Sunday morning. Parked three pews back in yet another church service, I held my head in my hands, probably leading some to think I was praying, which I was not. My shoulders were hunched over by despair, which draped around me like a damp blanket, but I couldn't think why. I had committed no great sin, and even doubt, that familiar killjoy foe that often stalks me during Christian gatherings that are high on certainty, was not the source of my struggle. But my heart was heavy.

The smiling greeters had been warm and welcoming enough; the worship band was skillful and enthusiastic without resorting to cheerleading or insisting we all burble with endless ecstasy, or sing that amazing song thirty-five more times. So why the niggle that buzzed around my brain like a pesky mosquito that resisted all swatting? When at last we passed the post of the final 'Amen', I was left with a feeling of breathless claustrophobia, exhausted by the experience and feeling more like a refugee than a family member. Why?

Reflecting later, I decided that things had gone seriously wrong during the preaching. The speaker said nothing that was theologically controversial, and I had no qualms about his sincerity. On the contrary, he had seemed utterly, unnervingly sincere. But hope had drained from me as he had painted the Christian life as endlessly *epic*. He described a life with Jesus as being more exciting, with more hairpin turns and stunning happenings than the entire *Mission Impossible* movie series. He had urged the congregation to expect more of God's activity in their everyday lives, to become full-time 'conduits of power', so that not only would goodness and mercy follow them all the days of their lives, but amazing happenings would follow in their wake, as they met children at the school gate, popped into the post office or shopped for some soup, stunning events every hour would pepper their daily existence. At first glance, there was nothing much wrong with that.

I was wearied by the suggestion that every day has to sparkle with significance, and be punctuated with messages from God and miraculous happenings. Life, including life for the Christian, includes plenty of dull days that can be filed away under the heading of 'Not much happened'. I'm not suggesting that God is distant or uninvolved; He is certainly not the deist deity who has started the universe with a word and then retreated for a few billion years to watch the result. Cliff Richard and Bette Midler were wrong when they sang of a God who is watching from a distance.

But God isn't a bottled genie who fixes every scrape or a chatterer who endlessly blathers in our ear about trivia. And if healing miracles are as freely available as the preacher suggested, then we should cancel a few services and head for the nearest cancer ward. Much as I'd like to live every day in the spiritual equivalent of a five-star resort, there are seasons when we all feel like we're languishing in the bleak landscape of a simmering wilderness. Mother Teresa, who gave of herself so heroically in serving the poor and dying in Calcutta, admitted that for thirty years she had sensed little of the presence of God. Writing to her friend, Michael van der Peet, she confessed, 'The silence and the emptiness is so great, that I look and do not see, listen and do not hear.'

Her days were heroic, but not always epic, if epic means supernatural.

Don't get me wrong. I believe in epic days. I became a Christian partly because of a miraculous healing, and I am in ministry because a guest speaker prophesied over me – and God told him my first and last name, which is anything but vague. I drove my car off the side of a cliff once, and my screaming turned to laughter when the car was somehow lifted back onto the road by an invisible hand. Don't think that I'm trying to handcuff God or render Him impotent, or worse still tag Him as disinterested. It's just that I also know that there are days, weeks and sometimes even decades where not much happens.

And then I realised that the preacher was projecting his life experience onto the congregation – he was travelling around to conferences, prayer gatherings and summit meetings with other leaders. And so he thundered that we should 'rise up and shift the atmosphere in the nation' – we were going to 'break through', if we 'secured our inheritance, and embraced our prophetic destiny'. Eh? What does all that mean on a Monday morning to the man who makes widgets in a factory or cleans the toilets in a motorway service stop?

And even those who do live in the world of Christian events don't live endlessly thrilled. This morning, I didn't wake up, do a triple back flip through the air, catching my tambourine as I flew, landing in my cowboy boots with a cry of 'Hallelujah'. Jesus has washed my sins away, but I still have to clean the car, get stuck on the M25, cough when I have a cold and get nervous when the credit card bill arrives.

So is God still in the miracle working business? Absolutely. But one of the greatest miracles of all, is to see ordinary followers of Jesus, doing ordinary and sometimes dishwater-dull tasks with excellence and faithfulness. The Irish novelist Colum McCann is right: it takes courage to live the ordinary life.

26. Named

Her name is on the trophy, and so it will remain, for a whole year, until next year's eagerly awaited competition. *Kay. 2011.* It's displayed in a very public place, proud testimony to her triumph.

It was 11pm, and we stumbled into the pub/bed and breakfast following a delightful evening with some Baptists in Worcester. Now we were ready for a snack, and a welcome sleep, but the pub had stopped serving food an hour earlier. Perhaps it was the pathetic, pleading look in our eyes as we ordered two packets of crisps, but the landlord decided to have mercy on us and open the kitchen again. Minutes later, he placed in front of us a plate of delicious sandwiches with bowls of piping hot soup and, smiling, offered us an unexpected invitation.

'We've got our annual conker competition happening in a few minutes. It's a big deal around here. Would you like to join in?' To be honest, I wasn't that thrilled at the idea. I was tired, and in an instant remembered that, as a child, I usually only managed to hit myself with my own conker. If you swing hard and miss, the conker often ploughs into your own forearm, bringing embarrassment and bruises. But there was something irresistible about his kindness, so we agreed. And so began an amazing couple of hours.

The locals welcomed us into their circle like old friends. In precompetition chatter and during the event itself, they asked us about our lives and seemed to really want to know. They included us in their jokes and subjected us to the friendly banter that usually only happens when you feel at ease in vintage friendships. There was one man who always wins, every year, the reigning, consistent champion. He got knocked out in the quarter finals, but laughed cheerfully, without a hint of chagrin.

At last, at 1am, it came down to the final: and, embarrassingly, it featured the two outsiders – Kay and me. As my conker shattered into four pieces, demolished by Kay's unexpected prowess, she was crowned Conker Queen of Worcester. Well, Conker Queen of that particular pub in Worcester. But the real highlight of the evening was the way the landlord had introduced us to the locals. 'Ladies and gentlemen, this is Jeff and Kay, and they're our guests tonight. I'm delighted that they've agreed to take part in our little competition. As our honoured guests, they can go first.'

Jeff and Kay. He used our names, and for the rest of the evening the locals did too. It seemed strange but rather wonderful hearing strangers call us by name. Dale Carnegie was right: a person's name is to him or her the sweetest and most important sound in any language. No one dreams of becoming whatsisname.

When someone uses my name, I know that they're talking with me, not at me, that they have noticed that I am really there. The use of a name creates intimacy and warmth. They've made the effort to remember. When I hear my name spoken, I know that I am more than just a number, a customer, a guy in the crowd, that bloke over there.

Two thousand years ago, a distraught woman, shattered by grief, met a man who she thought was a gardener. Much is made of the fact that she didn't recognise Him, the triumphant, resurrected Christ. But all that changed when He spoke one word to her.

'*Mary.*'

There are so many things He could have said. Considering all He'd been through, and the universe-altering victory He'd just won, He could have made the conversation all about Him.

'It's me. I've won. I've been to hell and back, literally. Death is sorted for good, don't you know? Everything is utterly different now.'

Instead, Jesus just spoke *her* name. Perhaps there was something in the pronunciation of it that was intimate, personal. But she remembered who He was because He remembered who she was. Elsewhere, greater signs had to help people recognise Jesus: a miraculous catch of fish. The breaking of bread following the meeting on the Emmaus Road. But just one word remade Mary's world, and that word was the sound of her own name.

Surely, as we endeavour to love and speak the good news, we need to remember to use people's names as we share it. People don't want to become our evangelistic projects, less still 'souls' that we count like scalps, notches on some evangelistic belt. They want to know if we want to know them, or whether we just want them to know Jesus.

And the mention of Mary's name says this: Easter is personal.

Every Easter, we affirm our faith: *Christ has died, Christ is risen, Christ will come again.* I've spent nearly forty years as a Christian, and so I'm over-familiar with the routine. After four decades of paschal greetings, sometimes the resurrection becomes a vague, pallid notion, a dusty doctrine that I affirm on Easter Sunday but one that makes little difference to my Easter Monday. At times, it seems like wishful thinking, the idea that death could be beaten. Grieving the loss of a close relative recently, I struggled with the fear that my hope of heaven for her, and for a reunion to come, was just pie-in-the-sky thinking. From here to eternity sometimes feels like a very great distance. And it's easier to believe in a resurrection generally, but not a resurrection for me specifically.

And so I need to have a sense, not only that Jesus is risen, but that in His resurrection, He whispers my name. Jeff. Mary. And your name too.

Meanwhile, in a pub in Worcester, there sits a tiny plastic trophy with a sticker plastered on it. *Kay. 2011.* And somewhere, because of Easter, there is a book, called the Lamb's Book of Life. It is filled with names. By grace, my name is there. And yours too.

Christ is risen. Hallelujah.

27. Look, Daddy

It was just a day trip into disability, nothing more.

I was in a wheelchair. Overzealous with some heavyweight bags, I'd insisted on lugging them both, until I felt something like a guitar string snap in my leg. I leapt around for a few minutes, praising the Lord. Well, something like that.

A few calls to the NHS helpline led to a trip to the casualty department of my local hospital, where I waited for three days to be seen.

OK, I exaggerate. It just felt like three days, even if it was only three hours. I tried to pass the time by guessing the maladies of the other bored looking patients in the waiting area, but the novelty of that soon wore off. When at last I saw a doctor, my worst fears were not realised, because this was not the twanging of my Achilles tendon, but just a torn calf muscle. I would use crutches for a few days, just to take the weight off. But another transatlantic flight was scheduled, and steering through airports would be impossible. Wheelchair assistance would be needed.

Feeling like a total fraud, I hobbled up to check in, and waited for the smiling man with the wheelchair. Almost immediately, it began. As soon as I sit in a wheelchair, I become invisible.

I immediately notice that some people talk *about* me, but not *to* me.

'Where is he going?' they ask each other, as if I have been robbed of my ability to speak, and not just torn a muscle.

I sit there, clutching my boarding pass and passport, and believe me, I know my own destination, but nobody asks. I have become an object rather than a subject. After a couple of hours of this, I find that I am quieter than usual, perhaps behaving as I feel I am expected to behave. Incredibly, I start to think that, if I spoke up, I might scare people. Yikes. He has a voice.

The two lovely people responsible for shunting me from one gate to another begin to flirt over the top of my head, and I begin to pray that their relationship will not go too much deeper in my presence. Pausing to pick up coffee, I wonder if one of them is going to use my head as a convenient place to balance her cup, so inanimate have I become.

At last we reach the plane, and a flight attendant smiles benignly at me with a grin usually reserved for small children. She slows down just a little when she speaks, her carefully annunciated words too loud. I silently celebrate that she doesn't pat me on the head and offer me a lolly.

During my brief excursion as a wheelchair user, there are some beautiful moments too. The man who helped me onto the plane had no patronising hint in his voice, just exemplified unbridled kindness and nothing-is-too-much generosity.

My day in a wheelchair gave me just the tiniest, fractional hint of what it might feel like to do life sitting down. It was obviously nothing like the reality. I always knew that within hours, my need for a wheelchair would be over. I had no sense of the horizon that hems disabled people in, every moment of every day. Mine was a momentary taste at the indignities they suffer.

But it was an amazing experience, and perhaps one that should be placed on the national curriculum. My greatest frustration was this:

I was not noticed. For the most part, I lived unseen. It was as if I had diminished in presence.

The security officer checked my passport, and chattered to the man who pushed me; a conversation took place that was literally over my head. Excuse me: *I'm* here.

The need to be seen is primal in all of us. Mummy, look at me, says the three-year-old. Daddy, watch me. And the wise parent notices, and greets the tottering new ballet step, the chaotic painting or the poo successfully landed in the potty with a round of applause. Foolish is the parent who fails to notice, and acknowledge that they are noticing.

At Christmas, we celebrate the God who sees us. He sees the whole crowd but picks each one of us out of it. But He does more than smile and wave.

The seeing Christ came down, from the unspeakable reaches of forever into the muck and mire of here and now. The true splendour of the season is this: we have been noticed, and rescue has come. Forget swirling snowflakes, carrot-nosed snowmen and benevolent Santas, all fat and white beards. Scrap the greeting card scene, all dewy-eyed cows and Eeyore donkeys, the stable softly lit.

'The cattle are lowing, the Baby awakes. But little Lord Jesus, no crying He makes.'

Why not? Why can't He cry?

No room at the inn. The stable stinks; it's a most unhygienic place to be born. A ragamuffin gaggle of shepherds show up, confused by bright lights and angel song in the night sky. A young husband holds his head in his hands, bewildered that God has planted a seed in his fiancée's virgin womb, but has omitted to book them a room.

He sees us. Rejoice!

And as we celebrate that God sees us, every one of us, let's be like Him, look around and notice.

28. Dangerous passion

The moment I set eyes on him, I knew I was in trouble. He was a religious smart missile. An intuitive alarm in my head wailed a warning: he was locked onto me, and was closing in fast. Zealous Christians don't walk – they march in strident resolution. I braced myself for impact. His jaw was set and his face was grim, his eyes wide and ablaze.

He collided without an introduction. 'I'm deeply concerned about the spiritual health of this event,' he said, the syllables staccato and crisp, his brow seemingly furrowed by years of practised frowning.

'I'm prayerfully concerned that people here are more interested in having fun than they are in seeking the living, holy God.' He paused for breath, and I knew what was coming next. Some passionate Christians are gunfighters for God, quick on the draw with biblical bullets. 'First Peter calls us to holiness, not levity. I'm deeply offended by the frivolity that is going on here. God is surely grieved.'

Deep inside, I sighed the sigh that sweeps through my soul like a tsunami when, every now and again, I want to abandon Christianity once and for all. My despair wasn't created because this man was nervous or even hostile about laughter. We're all different, and he doesn't have to enjoy humour as I do. That's a matter of preference. And it wasn't that I was worried that he had joined the ranks of the frozen chosen types who carefully arrange their facial muscles to look like they're in need of bran. My drowning sensation was created because I knew that, once again, I was talking to a passionately committed Christian. A crash helmet might be advisable.

Passionate Christians can be highly dangerous. I've reached this awkward conclusion after too many years of pastoral leadership.

Most of the church tribulations that I've witnessed have been created, not by nonchalant inquirers on the fringe of the church or by casual Christians who treat their faith like a weekend hobby. No, the uncomfortable truth is that I've seen people wounded, churches split, and lives ruined by sold out, white-hot, do-or-die zealots. It is the keen ones we need to watch.

Of course, I'm not calling for mediocrity. Christian discipleship is a passionate business, an invitation to die that we might live, a radical call to follow the Jesus whose stomach is turned by the lukewarm of Laodicea. But our passion can so easily become infected, and turn ugly. And none of us are immune.

Misguided zeal is an equal-opportunity virus, and it often strikes when a Christian begins a blinkered obsession with a single issue. Before long, they become monochrome extremists, every conversation a campaign speech. Their concern might matter greatly, but soon it matters exclusively.

The fire-breathing judgmental type insists that God is trembling with anger, His finger permanently poised above the smite button, and insists that the language of grace is disguised liberal compromise.

The charismatic warfare warriors love to rebuke something, somewhere before breakfast, and seem to believe that God is a ten pin bowler, judging by the number of times they fall over.

The social activist who sits arms folded in the worship service, nostrils flared with indignation, dismissing adoration as pious irrelevance.

And don't forget the intercessor, who prays mightily but quickly judges those who don't gather for the early morning prayer meeting.

So let's be passionate disciples – and that means passionate learners. Let's listen and not rant, or dismiss those who disagree with us as lesser mortals, pathetically impoverished because they're not as deep as us. Let's read books written by those we disagree with, and finish the book to find out if we really disagree. Let's realise that we can be wrong, and often are.

Meanwhile, the agitated complainant was insisting that God was prepping thunderbolts to hurl in my direction, and all because I didn't share his point of view. I tried to introduce a little warmth to the conversation by proffering what I thought was a witty quip, which was like cupping my hands around a piece of frozen chicken. This guy was not for turning. Or smiling. Or thawing.

And so on he went, on his deeply passionate, committed and apparently unhappy way. I looked up into the clear blue sky, and nervously scanned the horizon.

Not a thundercloud in sight.

29. Celebrity Christians

It's a tag that is increasingly used as a label of shame. Those to whom it is stuck can be seen as hungry for fame, superficial, self-promoting and diva like. It's a shorthand saying, but I can understand why the saying has come into vogue. Here's the label: *Christian celebrities*.

We're a culture obsessed with celebrity. Entire rain forests have succumbed to provide the paper for a myriad magazines that do nothing else than follow in the footsteps of the famous. Some mega-celebs have even launched their own magazines, literary altars to their own existence. Oprah Winfrey has *O, the Oprah Magazine*, and Katie Price aka Jordan, famous, as far as I know, for being famous, has the imaginatively titled glossy *Katie*. We have people who not only cook, but are celebrities because they're handsome and cheeky like Jamie, or swear and are abusive to their workers like Gordon. We have singing competitions judged by people who can't sing, but apparently know about music simply because they're famous.

And so, weary of hollow celebrities, there are some who point to well-known Christians, curl their lips, turn their faces into a sneer and label them as Christian celebrities. Recently, a letter appeared in a Christian magazine, screaming in shrill tones about the dangers of the Christian celebrity culture. In it, I was named, alongside dear friends like Steve

Chalke and Rob Parsons, as an example of celebrity. The writer said that we need to abandon well-known faces and voices and find people less known and tell their stories. It was inappropriate, the letter stated, to describe someone as an international speaker or television presenter. The letter was a warning, suggesting that something was very wrong indeed with the church world.

All of which tires me out. I totally agree that there is a need to share the treasured stories of those as yet unfamiliar to us. And I confess that it is worrying that most of the high-profile worship leaders around the world are handsome or beautiful souls whose facial arrangements look pretty good on the album cover. Thankfully, preachers are not required to be eye candy, which is a relief to me, although being attractive hasn't done Steve Chalke any harm.

But to tag those whose faces are familiar as celebrities, simply because they are well known is a cheap stunt. They are well known because a number of people, around the country, or around the world, have found their ministry/preaching/writing helpful. They have offered their lives to influence for the kingdom of God, just as anyone who serves Jesus does. As it turns out, because of the appreciation of the people of God, the blessing of God or, hopefully, a combination of the two, they have become familiar faces. People like to read their books and hear their Bible teaching. What's so very wrong with that?

It's too easy – and perhaps gratifying – to lob Christians whose names are known into a skip labelled 'celebrity'. It lines them up with PR created airheads in our wider world whose only talent is grabbing at headlines. To be tagged 'celebrity' implies that there is no real reason why our voices are listened to, that the familiar name is a person without experience or substance.

Being an unfamiliar name carries no intrinsic merits. And of course, there is the cycle of danger – as you profile someone's work, you risk the possibility that people might be interested in them or inspired by them – thus making them into potential 'celebrities'. Another candidate for the skip: people are starting to like them too much, so chuck them in quick. Is it right to make someone into a villain because they are popular?

It's OK to be well known if you're a legend (Billy Graham), or dead (Wilberforce and Mother Teresa), but for others in whom the Christian public show interest, there's no way out.

And why is it so wrong to be an *international* speaker? What's so terrible about having a passion to see the Church across the globe strengthened and encouraged? It's of no greater worth than being a local preacher, but it still has worth. And it was stated that it is wrong to use the term 'television presenter'. As one who is not (I have a face for radio), why is it a problem to be in that profession?

All this said, I do think there's some merit in the warning about Christian celebrities – and that should be to those who are privileged to have wide influence. They should not be condemned because of their profile, but certainly be held accountable for their attitude. When a Christian speaker/worship leader starts to act like a big fish in the tiny goldfish bowl that is the Christian world, demanding special treatment, projecting a nauseating air of pomposity and self-importance, then it's time to speak up. But let's demand humility and servanthood from the well-known, and not just throw bricks at them because they're well known.

Sometimes, in the Church, we're not too kind to each other. We snap at leaders because they fail, when their churches don't grow or their sermons are dull, and we snap at them because they bring a message that seems to help many, because their churches grow, and because their preaching and teaching makes an impact. In the Church, sometimes, it feels that you just can't win. And there's something very wrong with that.

30. Believing

A depressing drizzle kept my windscreen wipers in work as I turned into the church car park. There were plenty of spaces to choose from, a welcome sight at a Saturday morning pay and display, but not at a Sunday evening church event when you're the speaker and you've travelled a long way. The handful of cars said it all – not many people were going to show up tonight. Some speakers say that they don't care if the crowd is small. Either they lie or have graduated to a level of sainthood that is way beyond me. Communicating with a gaggle of souls, spread thinly around a cavernous building, can be torturous.

The organiser hurried out to the car to greet me, which was kind, considering the frigid weather. 'Hello, Jeff,' he smiled. 'Glad you made it OK. We don't have much of a crowd yet, but don't worry ... *I'm believing* that we'll have a full house 15 minutes from now.'

My facial muscles started to create my 'sure, look up there, there's a pig coming in to land' expression, but I caught them just in time, and nodded. But his 'I'm believing' language suddenly made me feel like an outsider looking in on Planet Christian, an all-too-frequent feeling of dislocation. How fragile I am: five minutes earlier, I had been praying while driving, eagerly asking God to make the evening purposeful. Now, as my host insisted that he was 'believing' for a last-minute stampede, I felt despair seep into my heart like a dose of rising damp.

When Christians plan events, but then Christian people are in short supply, out come the slogans and clichés. I've heard them all.

'It doesn't matter that there are only fifteen people in this 2,000-seat auditorium. The people that the Lord wants to be there will be there.' Really? So the low attendance is actually God's fault, because those who didn't come were eternally predestined not to show, which makes publicity a waste of time, because those whom God wants to be there will be there anyway. I don't think so. 'Don't give up the habit of meeting together' said the writer to the Hebrews, who responded (if they believed this notion): 'It's alright, if we don't bother, it's all in the plan.'

And there's the frequent flier prayer that is often spotted in pre-service prayer meetings: 'We thank You, Lord, that where two or three gather in Your name, there You are in the midst,' which is a biblical truth thinly disguised, showing that we're only expecting two or three human beings, but cheer up, because God will be there: He's promised it, and omnipresence guarantees that the promise will be honoured.

But it's the *really believing* bit that vexes me. What does it mean to *really* believe for something? Does believing just involve saying a sentence out loud, like, 'We'll have a full house', when it's patently obvious that we won't? Does *really* believing require me to thank God for doing something before He's actually done it? That seems like trying to embarrass God into doing what I want Him to do – a bit like sending a thank you card for the generous Christmas gift on December 4th. Sometimes the language of believing sounds perilously like wishing upon a star, crossing our fingers or just hoping for the best.

Some Christians apparently think that believing means intensity and lots of shouting. There's even a Facebook version of this. Someone posts that they're feeling under the weather (or near death), whereupon an assortment of very keen Christians respond with comments written in capital letters.

'SATAN, I REBUKE YOU IN THE NAME OF JESUS, AND DECLARE THAT FRED IS WHOLE AND WELL RIGHT NOW, I SAID *RIGHT* NOW, IN JESUS' NAME!!!!'

Bizarrely, this not only implies that Satan is a member of Facebook, and is therefore in a position to receive the rebuking status update, but also that demons flee and sickness scurries away whenever Christians get serious enough to start typing in capital letters. ('Oh no!' yelled the devil, obviously in great agony, 'No one told me that they were going to use UPPER CASE and even *ITALICISED* text on their social networking pages ...')

Surely believing means that we ask Jesus to intervene, and that we keep on asking, at least until it seems obvious that He is not going to intervene, at least in the way we'd prefer. Believing means that I refuse to walk sulkily away from Him when He is silent. Believers stand with each other in prayer and comfort during the wintry seasons of drizzly doubt; they worship when there's no other apparent reason to worship than this: He is worthy. Believing is not about working ourselves into a religious lather, but knowing that as we declare, in liturgy or song, that He is the resurrection and the life, we'll start to believe it a little more. Believing calls us to rest in the conviction that we are greatly loved, and that the blathering on at Him that we call insistent prayer doesn't irritate, but delights Him. Believing means that we'll be realistic, but not cynical. We'll pray for the best, and prepare for the worst.

And believing faith is never sleek and perfect. One of my favourite biblical characters is the chap who, challenged by Jesus with the potential of believing, cried, 'Lord, I believe. Help me overcome my unbelief.' It was partial, limping faith, trust that Jesus didn't curl His lip at. A miracle happened, even though faith was flawed: perhaps it always is.

31. Something for the weekend

Church weekends aren't what they used to be. I've been to Christian conference centres where, terrifyingly, one received electric shocks when climbing into the bath (at no extra charge), where dinner time was lightened by the playing of the 'Name that Food' game (because what was on the plate was quite unrecognisable as being something for human consumption), and where the waiting staff were so stern, one suspects they were thrown out of the Gestapo for being too rough. Failure to stack one's dirty plates at the end of the meal could result in death by stoning, or so the stony glares from the waitresses threatened.

I've slept on beds that had probably served in medieval torture chambers, in bedrooms that were so cold they could have been ideal for the training of missionaries to the Antarctic.

Things have changed, for the most part. These days, just about every Christian conference centre I know does a marvellous job on limited budgets.

But even in the bad old days, remarkable things happened during those weekends away. I received a very clear call to ministry at the first one I attended. I'd only been a Christian for just a few weeks, and, incredibly, had been sensing a call to Christian leadership, and especially preaching and teaching, which was remarkable, seeing as I didn't know the difference between the Old Testament, the New Testament and the maps at the back of both testaments. I've written elsewhere about what happened, so won't repeat myself here, but suffice it to say it was probably the clearest, most stunning encounter with God of my life – and it happened during that weekend away. I had a similar experience at youth camps, and despite the fact that I was overly keen which led to some silliness on my part – I'd respond to every sermon by going forward, whatever the substance of the 'altar call' – those days were incredibly formative for me.

But it's not just about God speaking at these church weekends. There's great beauty and blessing as the people of God speak to each other. In our busy lives, where most of us battle 'quickaholism', we can end up having close encounters of a Christian kind on Sunday mornings that are, actually, anything but close. Christian ships passing in the morning, we mutter our greetings and hurried summaries of the highs and lows of our week, and chatter quickly at the end of the service, but often there's no time to build friendships of substance. During those weekends away, relationships are cemented as people laugh and often cry together. Confessions are made which means that the retreat, far from being an opportunity to be far from the madding crowd, turns into a life-changing junction. Cups of tea made, glasses of wine shared, tears wept: all these moments help build a church together, and a weekend away together can accelerate a depth of fellowship that might take years without it.

And during these weekends away, we usually discover that we, like everyone else, are just frail humans, which is good, because arriving on a Friday evening to a church weekend can be daunting. Everyone else seems to have shoals of fish on the backs of their cars, and they were probably singing hymns during the journey as opposed to swearing on the M25. To know that everyone else is in the process is helpful, as sometimes even the name of the weekend away itself can be intimidating, if it suggests that revival is definite, or revolution of any kind is likely.

At one weekend away, I met a lady who confessed to me that she had taken her family to a car wash, whereupon the drivers' window fell all the way down inside the car door, meaning that everyone would be drowned. How relieved and thrilled I was to learn that her solution to this dilemma was to insert her own bottom into the window to create an airtight seal, thus preventing her family from experiencing anything close to a Noah and the flood experience. She could have just backed out of the car wash ... but then, I suppose, that's exactly what she did do.

Thank God for church weekends away. They can be eternity-changing.

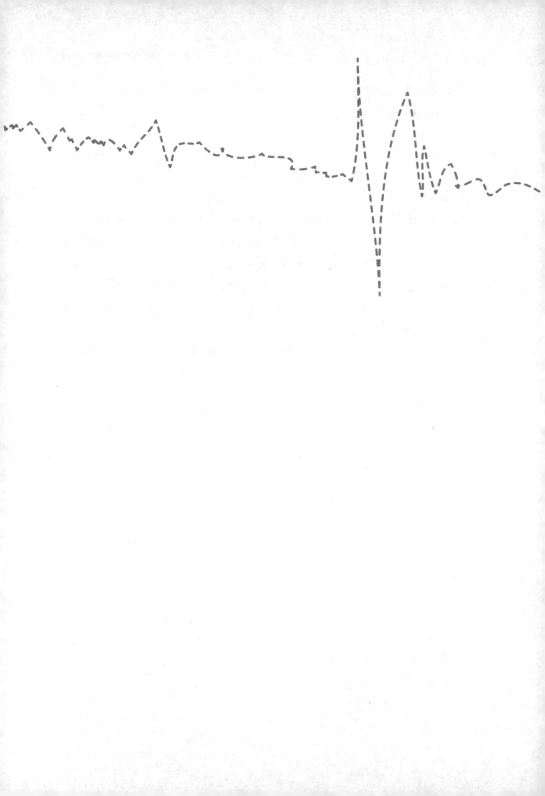

32. He's not nervous

Perilous places are usually posted with warning signs; a skull and crossbones for the toxic, and the ominous yellow and black triad that indicates radiation. The word 'DANGER!' shouts loud in capital letters, further amplified by the '!' at the end. And 'Achtung!' prevents Germans from straying into something nasty.

Australia is beautiful, but the whole country should carry a health warning. In the last 48 hours, I've encountered some seriously dodgy critters. Crocodile Lucas, that's me.

Scuba diving the Great Barrier Reef meant wearing a 'stinger' suit to protect from a lethal caress – the tentacles of the box jellyfish. I found myself in the company of a giant snapper clam, three stingrays and a couple of reef sharks that looked eager to snack. I had something in common with the sharks – both they and I were praying. My gurgled underwater intercessions were begging for protection. I think the sharks were getting truly thankful for what they were about to receive.

Venturing on safari into the inhospitable, gloomy rainforest, I unwittingly gave blood, and without the reward of the usual cup of tea and a biscuit, as some leeches attached themselves to my legs. Leeches suck, literally, and make Henry VIII look like Twiggy, growing to ten times their usual size after the leech equivalent of a decent curry.

And the world's most dangerous bird, the cassowary, was in the thick undergrowth. It looks emu-cute, but like the velociraptor in *Jurassic Park*, they like to lunge at humans with razor-sharp claws, disembowelling them, which isn't nice. There were killer plants that sting like twelve bees if touched; and then I came just one step away from a deadly snake, the red belly-black, also known by its natty Latin name, *pseudechis porphyriacus*. I screamed so loud, other visitors in the forest probably thought that a cassowary had jabbed a victim in the intestines. Shocked, I hollered, 'Oh, *pseudechis porphyriacus!*' Or something similar.

But in the midst of all these perils, all was well, or so I thought, because our trusty guide seemed supremely cool and confident. As long as he was with us, we were in safe hands. As we traversed a croc-infested, swollen river in his Land Rover, water up over the wheel arches, I casually remarked that he must be used to these extreme jungle-like conditions. Alarmingly, he shook his head.

'Actually, no, Jeff. Sometimes I lie awake at night, unable to sleep, anxious about what could go wrong during one of these trips.' I laughed out loud, a high pitched squeal – the Aussies are so funny, I mused. Then I realised he wasn't joking. Suddenly my sense of safety evaporated. In the land of 'no worries', my guide was very worried, so how anxious should I be? Blood drained from my face, and not just because the leeches were working overtime. As a newcomer in the jungle, you're only as strong as your guide.

Life is a shadowland loaded with perils. Jesus posts the starkest warning sign: 'In this world, you'll have trouble.' But then He answers a thousand questions with the promise: 'I am with you – always.'

He's seen it all. And He isn't worried. He's been tested with multiple temptations and passed with perfect scores. He's promised to be faithful, with us, always. This doesn't have to be a lonely planet.

His being with us doesn't mean we'll be without pain. But when suffering looms, we won't have to square up to it alone. When the terrifying tentacles of death swirl around us, we're assured of this: the sting has been removed. He'll walk us through our final breaths, and escort us to a new kind of Jerusalem.

Sometimes I sense His presence; a coincidence that faith realises is answered prayer; a scintillating moment during worship. And then there are days, months even, when He seems far away. Is He there, and if He is, is He interested? Whatever my emotions, I affirm this truth, which works better when I declare it in the company of others: 'Even though I walk through the valley of the shadow of death, You are with me.' His power works within me. The toughest days can become a classroom. New discoveries await.

And speaking of discoveries, these recent adventures mean I have uncovered another highly dangerous species, while out on the dive-boat. A muscly German sun-worshipper lathered himself with coconut-scented chip fat, and was on the fast track to becoming a lobster. I sat downwind of him while eating a very crumbly blueberry muffin. A gust came up and, to my horror, he became a coated, pebbledashed person, *Germanicus inder breadcrumbs*. He was not thrilled.

Yikes. Achtung indeed.

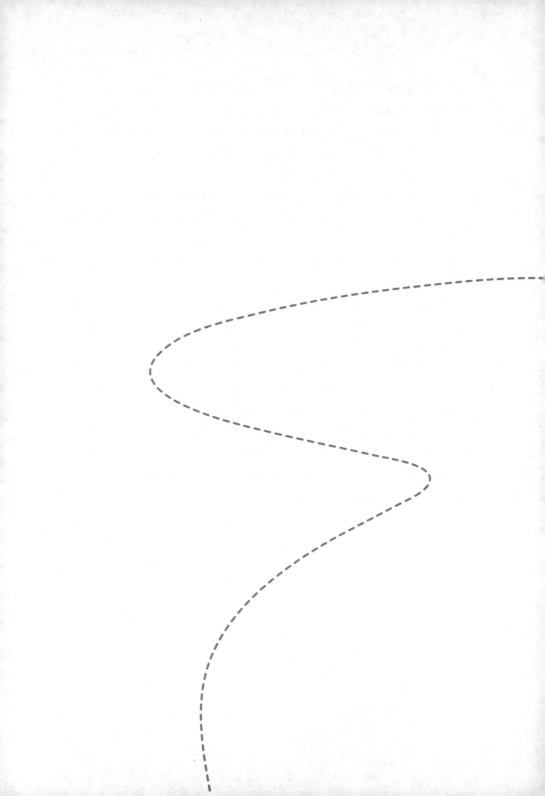

33. The $64,000 question

We call it the listening test.

It's a little game that Kay and I like to play.

No, this is not about eavesdropping on other people's conversations when in public places, like on trains, and in restaurants, although that is another of our furtive little hobbies. Occasionally, when we go out for a meal, Kay actually tilts her head to one side (apparently this enables better listening), which is a little obvious. Recently, while sharing a fine Chicken Pasanda, I suggested buying surveillance equipment for her birthday, which would enable her to tune in more effectively. She hushed me to be quiet, as the conversation unfolding at the next table was utterly epic and far more interesting than our own. She'd make a great spook, as in MI5, not ghost. My pet name for her is GCHQ.

But the listening test is what we sometimes apply when we meet new people, and we are suddenly thrust into a conversation. Travelling in ministry means that sometimes we're met at airports by someone that we've never met, who is holding a card that says 'Lucas', but, unhelpfully, not holding a balloon. We then get into their car, and the conversation – and the game begins. We discuss our journey: 'How was the flight?' It was as it normally is: we took off, we ate food unrecognisable as food, and we landed: the usual routine. We comment on the weather: good, bad, rainy, blisteringly hot. And then we start to ask about them – their background, church life, interests, family. But the acid test is this: will they ask anything much about us, and if they do and we start to tell them, will they be really interested and listen for long?

Call me jaundiced if you like, but I have a theory that most people don't really care and are not that interested beyond a few cursory pleasantries. That includes Christian people, which is a shame, because we're supposed to be known by our loving kindness. That means being interested, and is vital if we're ever going to be effective in mission, because people want to be cared about, and not just targeted as projects or prospects.

Perhaps we're all casualties of our own busyness. Or maybe it's a fruit of being buried in technology: we're more fascinated by staring at our iPhones and fighting off Angry Birds than we are in the fascinating story of another human being.

But for whatever reason, it's rare to find someone who has the priceless gift of listening, who doesn't treat conversation as a potential monologue, where your answer is simply an opportunity for them to take a breath before they hold court once again. Celebrated psychologist Paul Tournier memorably said, 'Listen to the conversations of our world, between nations as well as between couples. They are, for the most part, dialogues of the deaf.' Why is social networking such a successful phenomenon? It enables us to say what we think, report on what we're doing, even if what we're doing is cooking an omelette. We update our status in the hope that someone, somewhere, might be interested. We want to be known.

The scarcity of interest is a fabulous opportunity, not for us to fake love, but to show authentic care. The simple enquiry, 'Tell me more', can unlock a heart. People part with large sums of cash just to experience the fabulous luxury of being listened to.

A friend recently discovered how being interested can bring a sudden thaw to a chilly disposition. Out for breakfast, the waitress who served him was brisk and unfriendly. Noticing that she had a rather spectacular tattoo, he casually remarked, 'That looks great. Can you tell me about it?' Summer arrived in the face of the weary waitress, as she enthusiastically talked about the why of her tattoo.

Of course, showing genuine interest is not a guarantee of success.

Enthused by my friend's tattooed waitress story, a chap who worked in a motorbike store greeted a grumpy looking biker customer and decided to try his 'tell me more' experiment. 'That's an amazing tattoo you've got there, pal,' he gushed, 'can you tell me about it?'

'What the hell has it got to do with you?' grunted the biker.

You can't win them all. But we can win some, or at least make their day.

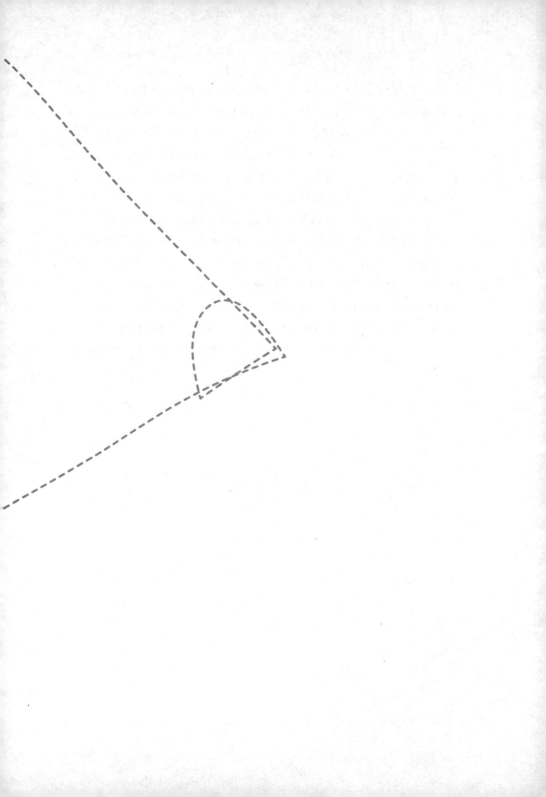

34. It can be done

It was about twenty years ago when I made what I thought was the final decision. I am not an athlete, I concluded, and so physical exercise would not be a part of my life. I would eat sensibly, drink moderately, but my ever-increasing shadow would not darken the doors of a gym. Those who worked out, I decided, were not mere mortals like me. And Olympic level competitors? They were demigods, epic souls to admire, but impossible to emulate.

This anti-fitness choice came after careful consideration of extensive data, like the fact that bending over to tie up my shoes took my breath away. And I had a long history of being rubbish at anything remotely sporty. I still blush crimson when I remember playing football during high school. Despite being placed in the defensive position of left back, I enthusiastically dashed all over the field for the first five minutes of the game, until our irate (and unnaturally chiselled) sports teacher blew his whistle and, punctuating his question with swear words, asked me what on earth I was playing at. I had no defence (literally), seeing as I was offside at the front of the field, instead of being dutiful at the back of the field. I knew back then that I'd never be able to bend anything like Beckham.

I hated rope climbing, mainly because I couldn't ever climb a rope.

It's a shame, because rope climbing was an Olympic event until 1932, and is threatening to make a comeback. Even though I was moved when I read about the gold medal winning performance of Olympian George Eyser, who won the rope climbing event in 1904 (and did it with just one wooden leg), I knew that even with two legs of my own, I'd be hopeless.

And I was a chaotic jumble of bouncing limbs on the trampoline. I'd come last in the cross-country run, and complain that oxygen was not provided. I was pretty good at cricket – when it came to keeping score, not playing. And so all of this led me to conclude: if sedentary living became an Olympic activity, I might stand a chance at victory but, until then, I had no hope.

All of which makes me wonder: in what other areas of my life have I hoisted a white flag of surrender, and submitted myself to a sentence of sameness? Have I unwittingly decided that, like the proverbial leopard, I can never change my spots? We all make endless decisions, most of them subconsciously, about what we can and cannot do. And so we write ourselves off from possibilities and potential. Where have we decided that everything might change, but we can't? Have we succumbed to that innocuous habit pattern, which is more annoying than perilous, or the silent staking of addiction, which doesn't send us an email to announce that we're trapped in its grasp?

We don't pray because we think we can't, we don't risk because we think it's not in our nature, we don't learn a new skill because we've decided it's too late. And often we're quite wrong. Some things that we think we can't do can be done.

Seven years ago I changed my mind about me. Today, I can only look at the gathering Olympians with admiration, but most days I run four miles. I lift weights, puff and pant on an elliptical, and hang upside down like a bat on an inverter, which is odd, but apparently has some benefits. I am healthier at fifty-five than I was at thirty-five, and it's due, in part, to my starting to believe that I could live differently. If anyone should believe that we can change, we Christians should. We're the ones who believe that change doesn't just come from gritted teeth and sweat, but that the same Spirit who raised Jesus from the dead is the transformer working within each of us.

I'm also pleased to report that I have managed to showcase my trampolining skills for royalty. Attending a youth club where Prince Phillip was visiting, we were told to follow two vital instructions: bow when you meet him, and then carry on doing whatever you're doing, because he wants to see a youth club in action. Bouncing away on the trampoline when the illustrious guest arrived, I was horrified when he headed directly to me, where my aerial display of flailing arms and legs akimbo was not a pretty sight. But I learned something about royal etiquette that day. It's very hard to bow and bounce at the same time.

But it can be done.

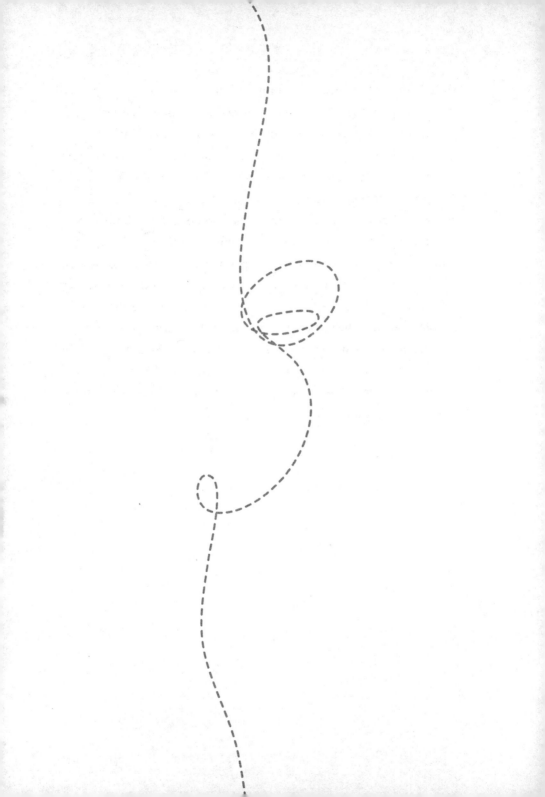

NATIONAL DISTRIBUTORS

UK: (and countries not listed below)

CWR, Waverley Abbey House, Waverley Lane, Farnham, Surrey GU9 8EP.

Tel: (01252) 784700 Outside UK (44) 1252 784700 Email: mail@cwr.org.uk

AUSTRALIA: KI Entertainment, Unit 21 317-321 Woodpark Road, Smithfield,
New South Wales 2164. Tel: 1 800 850 777 Fax: 02 9604 3699
Email: sales@kientertainment.com.au

CANADA: David C Cook Distribution Canada, PO Box 98, 55 Woodslee Avenue, Paris,
Ontario N3L 3E5. Tel: 1800 263 2664 Email: sandi.swanson@davidccook.ca

GHANA: Challenge Enterprises of Ghana, PO Box 5723, Accra.

Tel: (021) 222437/223249 Fax: (021) 226227 Email: ceg@africaonline.com.gh

HONG KONG: Cross Communications Ltd, 1/F, 562A Nathan Road, Kowloon.

Tel: 2780 1188 Fax: 2770 6229 Email: cross@crosshk.com

INDIA: Crystal Communications, 10-3-18/4/1, East Marredpalli, Secunderabad – 500026, Andhra
Pradesh. Tel/Fax: (040) 27737145 Email: crystal_edwj@rediffmail.com

KENYA: Keswick Books and Gifts Ltd, PO Box 10242-00400, Nairobi.

Tel: (020) 2226047/312639 Email: sales.keswick@africaonline.co.ke

MALAYSIA: Canaanland, No. 25 Jalan PJU 1A/41B, NZX Commercial Centre, Ara Jaya,
47301 Petaling Jaya, Selangor. Tel: (03) 7885 0540/1/2 Fax: (03) 7885 0545
Email: info@canaanland.com.my

Salvation Publishing & Distribution Sdn Bhd, 23 Jalan SS 2/64, 47300 Petaling Jaya, Selangor.

Tel: (03) 78766411/78766797 Fax: (03) 78757066/78756360
Email: info@salvationbookcentre.com

NEW ZEALAND: KI Entertainment, Unit 21 317-321 Woodpark Road, Smithfield, New South Wales
2164, Australia. Tel: 0 800 850 777 Fax: +612 9604 3699
Email: sales@kientertainment.com.au

NIGERIA: FBFM, Helen Baugh House, 96 St Finbarr's College Road, Akoka, Lagos.

Tel: (01) 7747429/4700218/825775/827264 Email: fbfm_1@yahoo.com

PHILIPPINES: OMF Literature Inc, 776 Boni Avenue, Mandaluyong City.

Tel: (02) 531 2183 Fax: (02) 531 1960 Email: gloadlaon@omflit.com

SINGAPORE: Alby Commercial Enterprises Pte Ltd, 95 Kallang Avenue #04-00, AIS Industrial
Building, 339420. Tel: (65) 629 27238 Fax: (65) 629 27235 Email: marketing@alby.com.sg

SOUTH AFRICA: Struik Christian Media, 1st Floor, Wembley Square II, Solan Street, Gardens, Cape
Town 8001, South Africa. Tel: +27 (0)21 460 5400 Fax: +27 (0)21 461 7662
Email: info@struikchristianmedia.co.za

SRI LANKA: Christombu Publications (Pvt) Ltd, Bartleet House, 65 Braybrooke Place, Colombo 2.
Tel: (9411) 2421073/2447665 Email: dhanad@bartleet.com

USA: David C Cook Distribution Canada, PO Box 98, 55 Woodslee Avenue, Paris,
Ontario N3L 3E5, Canada. Tel: 1800 263 2664 Email: sandi.swanson@davidccook.ca

CWR is a Registered Charity – Number 294387
CWR is a Limited Company registered in England Registration Number 1990308

Courses and seminars

Publishing and new media

Conference facilities

Transforming lives

CWR's vision is to enable people to experience personal transformation through applying God's Word to their lives and relationships.

Our Bible-based training and resources help people around the world to:
• Grow in their walk with God
• Understand and apply Scripture to their lives
• Resource themselves and their church
• Develop pastoral care and counselling skills
• Train for leadership
• Strengthen relationships, marriage and family life and much more.

Our insightful writers provide daily Bible-reading notes and other resources for all ages, and our experienced course designers and presenters have gained an international reputation for excellence and effectiveness.

CWR's Training and Conference Centre in Surrey, England, provides excellent facilities in an idyllic setting – ideal for both learning and spiritual refreshment.

Applying God's Word
to everyday life and relationships

CWR, Waverley Abbey House,
Waverley Lane, Farnham,
Surrey GU9 8EP, UK

Telephone: **+44 (0)1252 784700**
Email: **info@cwr.org.uk**
Website: **www.cwr.org.uk**

Registered Charity No 294387
Company Registration No 1990308

Life Every Day is written bimonthly by Jeff Lucas, to help you apply the Bible to your everyday life.

Through laughter and tears, and his customary wit and wisdom, Jeff will help you to gain daily insight, understanding and practical application from God's Word.

Expect to be challenged, encouraged and entertained!

1-year subscriptions available in print or by daily email.
Individual issues available in print or as eBooks.

For current prices and to order visit **www.cwr.org.uk/store**
Also available online or from Christian bookshops

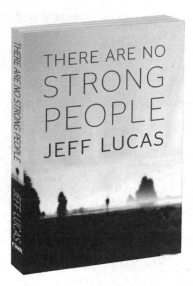

See Samson and your own life in a new light

Is it possible to be hugely blessed by God – and still make a mess of your life? In this provocative, breathtakingly honest book on the Bible's infamous rascal, Samson, Jeff Lucas explores some vital principles for living life well.

• What is it we all really crave?
• Do good people do bad things?
• What do we do when we're disappointed?
• Are there clear steps towards success – and disaster?

You will see Samson and your own life in a new light as you reflect on his journey.

There Are No Strong People
by Jeff Lucas
234-page paperback, 172x230mm
ISBN: 978-1-85345-624-4

Andy Robb's alter ego, the bumbling clergyman Derek the Cleric, is the vicar at St Cliff's. Enjoy a window into his wacky world with this collection of marvellous musings and hilarious letters, emails, 'Notes to Self' and clippings from St Cliff's Weekly News Sheet! Sure to entertain, Derek the Cleric is unforgettable!

'If you … ever start finding the fun has fallen out of your faith, you need a strong dose of Derek the Cleric.' – **Russ Bravo**

A Year at St Cliff's (Derek the Cleric)
by Andy Robb
144-page paperback, 130x175mm
ISBN: 978-1-85345-763-0

For current price and to order visit **www.cwr.org.uk/store**
Also available online or from Christian bookshops